—ROBYN WALENSKY—

BEAUTIFUL LIFE?

The CSI Behind the Casey Anthony Trial
& My Observations from Courtroom Seat #1

363.259523
W17J

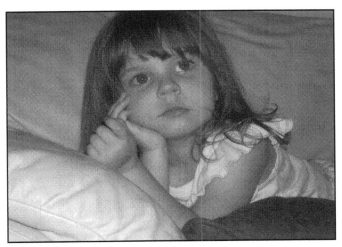

Caylee Anthony
"Florida State Attorney's Office, 9th Judicial Circuit"

INTRODUCTION

Another adorable girl, gone missing in America. The first time I see Caylee Anthony's picture on TV and hear she's missing, two faces flash in my mind. First up is the image of JonBenet Ramsey. Second, Natalee Holloway. Two terrible tragedies. Two murders that remain unsolved to date. Two cases of attractive American children that capture the world's attention on TV. The world will also come to know about the tragic short life of Caylee Marie Anthony. I followed the JonBenet Ramsey case from the start and covered it in Boulder, Colorado, when John Mark Karr confessed in Bangkok, Thailand, claiming he killed JonBenet. I've stood outside the stunning gingerbread-style home, what I call the "house of horrors" on Fifteenth Street in Boulder wondering who in the world could have murdered this child, and why. JonBenet struck in the head, strangled with a garrote, and the six-year-old may have been sexually assaulted by the creep who killed her. I reported on the Natalee Holloway case from Aruba. On the anniversary of her disappearance, as part of my news assignment, I take a room at the Holiday Inn Sunspree Resort in Palm Beach,

Aruba, where Natalee stays on her high school graduation trip, and I retrace her final steps. I also cover the grief from her hometown of Mountain Brook, Alabama, where neighbors and those who never knew Natalee tie yellow ribbons to trees. Natalee's picture is plastered all over the beach on the tourist island of Aruba. But her body has never been found. I am reminded of both cases when I visit the National Museum of Crime and Punishment in Washington, D.C., in the spring of 2011. Posters of the girls and their tragic stories appear in the COLD CASE section of the museum. The last page of the book on both crimes, the murder of JonBenet Ramsey and the murder of Natalee Holloway, have yet to be written. The same holds true for the murder of Caylee Marie Anthony. There is no video tape of the killer taking the life of the two-year-old. No knife. No gun. Only one person has a motive. But we may never know the exact sequence of events. The moment or moments of horror that led to Caylee taking her last breath may never be known, unless the killer confesses. Caylee's adorable face and body reduced to skull and bones. Her skin and smile gone. I look up at the TV monitor over my head in Courtroom #23. The prosecutor publishes the crime scene picture for the jury. I cringe. There is Caylee's small skull. Some of her hair is still there, stuck to the duct tape. The skull in a swamp full of mud, weeds, and vines. Although no one is supposed to make a sound in the courtroom, there is an audible gasp and many, including seasoned hard-core crime reporters look away. I do a double take, a triple take, and try to memorize every detail of the image so I can describe it for my radio audience. The reality of the photo is overwhelming. The reality of what happens to Caylee, unimaginable. The killer snuffing her out most likely with chloroform and wrapping duct tape over her little mouth and nose. The psycho, heartless killer putting a heart-shaped sticker over the duct tape on Caylee's mouth. A female touch, as if to say in some sick way: "I'm so sorry. I love you." A dead Caylee is triple bagged. Her small body put callously in two garbage bags and a white laundry bag taken from the Anthony home. Prosecutor Jeff Ashton will call the laundry bag "Caylee's coffin." She is buried with her Winnie the Pooh blanket taken from her bedroom in the Anthony home. Then the stone-cold killer tosses her like trash into the woods, walking distance from the Anthony home. And just like the murders of JonBenet Ramsey and Natalee Holloway, a truly evil person kills Caylee Marie Anthony before she can live a beautiful life.

Caylee Anthony
"Florida State Attorney's Office, 9th Judicial Circuit"

AUTHOR'S NOTES

The Casey Anthony case is clearly the trial of this century. CSIs and detectives from the Orange County Sheriff's Office in Orlando, Florida, were first on scene and used high-tech investigative techniques to process the mountain of evidence as the case unfolded. Some of the science was introduced for the very first time in our nation's court system. In "Beautiful Life?" you will hear from the CSIs who collected air samples from the trunk of Casey's car, found the strand of hair and heart-shaped stickers, and photographed Caylee's remains in the woods. You will hear from the lead detectives who interrogated Casey Anthony at Universal Studios. The CSIs and detectives speak out for the first time in their own words. A majority of quotes come directly from one-on-one interviews conducted by reporter Robyn Walensky. Additional quotes are from direct testimony; Robyn Walensky's reporting and personal observations from jury selection at the Pinellas County Criminal Justice Center in Clearwater, Florida; and from WDBO Radio's front-row seat #1 in Courtroom 23 on the twenty-third floor of the Orange County Courthouse in Orlando, Florida. There are approximately four hundred pieces of evidence and one hundred witnesses, some who take the stand multiple times during the six-week trial. This is not a comprehensive look at every witness and every piece of evidence.

Beautiful Life? focuses on the CSI behind the case as told to Robyn Walensky by individual members of the Orange County Sheriff's Office who chose to participate in one-on-one interviews for this project. The book is a compilation of the highlights of the case. The book does not follow a strict timeline

Prior to the Casey Anthony trial, I attended the Orange County Civilian Police Academy and graduated from Class #61. For twelve weeks on Tuesday nights I took courses lasting up to four hours, which included lectures from members of the SWAT team, Forensics and Crime Scene Units, K-9, and Mounted Patrol. We took tours of the 9-1-1 Communications Center, the Supply and Uniform Unit, and the Crime Lab. WDBO Radio allotted me a Wednesday weekly 6:40 a.m. segment and I would report on what I learned "behind the scenes" at the Academy. The instructors included homicide detectives, robbery investigators, crime scene investigators, and undercover deputies working narcotics. Some of the speakers were directly involved in the Casey Anthony case. I came away with enormous insight into the workings of the department lead by Sheriff Jerry Demings who welcomed our class on night #1 and who presented us with our diplomas at graduation.

The front book cover photo is from a prosecution exhibit entered into evidence on June 10, 2011. Dr. Michael Warren, a University of Florida anthropology professor and human identification laboratory director, created the computer animation to show how the duct tape could have contributed to the death of Caylee Anthony.

The animation starts out with a picture of Caylee and Casey Anthony. Next a photo of Caylee's decomposed skull is put over the original image. Finally a picture of the duct tape recovered from the swamp scene found on the remains is superimposed over Caylee's face to show the single piece of tape is wide enough to easily cover Caylee's nose and mouth. Despite opposition from Casey's defense team, Judge Belvin Perry, Jr., allows the exhibit to be shown to jurors. Lead defense attorney Jose Baez calls for a mistrial based on the video, saying it's prejudicial and that it serves only one purpose, "to inflame the jury." Baez says, "This disgusting superimposition is nothing more than a fantasy…They're throwing things against the wall and seeing if it sticks." Warren testifies that in his opinion the duct tape found with Caylee's skull was placed there before her body began decomposing. Prosecutor Jeff Ashton will argue the video demonstrates a single piece of tape placed over Caylee's nose and mouth is enough to kill her.

The back cover picture of the Caylee memorial cross at the woods scene is from the personal photo collection of Orange County Sheriff's Office Crime Scene Supervisor Michael Vincent, taken July 20, 2011.

A portion of the proceeds is being donated to The Children's Safety Village, operated under the umbrella of the Orange County Sheriff's Office. The money is specifically being put toward finger-printing and DNA collection kits for children attending schools, day-care centers, churches, synagogues, and summer camps in Orange County, Florida.

Children's Safety Village of Central Florida
is generously supported by

*This book is dedicated to the men and women
of the Orange County Sheriff's Office
who worked tirelessly for three years to solve the murder
of Caylee Marie Anthony.*

CONTENTS

CHAPTER 1

THE SCENE SPEAKS

"What does the Caylee remains crime scene say to you?"

**– WDBO radio reporter Robyn Walensky in an
interview with Orange County Sheriff's Office
Crime Scene Supervisor Michael Vincent**

"I get the phone call there's skeletal remains found around the corner
from the Anthony house, and right away I think it's the little girl."

– Crime Scene Supervisor Michael Vincent

"And the proximity to the home?" **– Robyn Walensky**

"I was amazed she was that close."

– Crime Scene Supervisor Michael Vincent

"And the killer?" **– Robyn Walensky**

"The killer clearly had no feelings, no emotion."

– Crime Scene Supervisor Michael Vincent

CHAPTER 2

OOH, OOH,
THAT SMELL

"I can't find my granddaughter. There is something wrong. I found my daughter's car today and it smells like there's been a DEAD BODY in the DAMN car!"

– Cindy Anthony to 9-1-1 Operator, July 15, 2008

"Human decomposition. It's strong and it's unique. And that particular smell, once you smell it for the first time in your life, you never forget that smell. Simple as that." **– CSI Geraldo Bloise**

"On the first whiff. I immediately, without a doubt, knew something dead had been in the trunk of the car."

– Crime Scene Supervisor Michael Vincent

It was so strong. There's no question, once I opened the door to the car, what that smell was. When people say it 'knocked them back,' I was taken aback by the smell. It was just as if you were to walk into an apartment where there was a dead body and you would smell that smell of decomposition of a body that had been there for a few days. There's no question what that smell was." **– Corporal Yuri Melich, lead detective on the case**

"As they approach the vehicle, an overwhelming smell is emanating from it and it's coming from the trunk. George Anthony will tell you that he said a silent prayer that it was neither his daughter nor his granddaughter...George Anthony got into that car, drove it home. When Cindy Anthony had her first contact with the car, her words to George Anthony were, 'Jesus, what died?'"
– Prosecutor Linda Drane Burdick during her opening argument

"There it is on national television. Casey's white car, a 1998 white Pontiac Sunfire, parked in the garage at the Orange County crime lab. In my mind, the most crucial piece of evidence for the prosecution in this case. I wonder how the media is able to get such great video of it." **– Robyn Walensky**

"That night, July 16 of 2008, with the permission of George and Cindy Anthony, the Orange County Sheriff's Office seized Casey Anthony's white Pontiac Sunfire. And you will hear testimony from crime scene technicians, and ultimately individuals who evaluated and analyzed evidence taken from that trunk during the course of this trial."

– Prosecutor Linda Drane Burdick during her opening argument

"The car was towed into the crime lab. The smell was so overwhelming when the trunk of the vehicle was opened, that I was concerned crime scene investigators would not be able to work in the office area the following day if the stench seeped into the office on the other side of the garage wall. So a decision was made to leave the garage door open."   **– Crime Scene Supervisor Michael Vincent**

"At least one photographer from a local Orlando TV station goes to the alley behind the fenced-in parking lot of the Orange County Sheriff's Office crime lab, gets up on top of the live truck, points the camera, and shoots the video of the white smelly Sunbird."

– Robyn Walensky

Casey's Car parked inside OCSO Crime Lab
"Florida State Attorney's Office, 9th Judicial Circuit"

"Later, after hearing the 9-1-1 call and listening to Cindy Anthony on the news say there was pizza in the trash bag that caused the smell, I went to the drying room where the trash was being kept. It was the first time I saw the trash and I got up close and personal and smelled it. There is absolutely no way the odor of decomp was coming from the trash." **– Crime Scene Supervisor Michael Vincent**

"I wonder at what point these seasoned detectives realize they have a possible baby killer on their hands. I put the question to veteran detective Sergeant John Allen." **– Robyn Walensky**

"For me, it was later that evening when we went into the forensics bay and I smelled the car. Once I smelled it, at that point, I felt like potentially we were looking at something other than a missing child. But clearly walking toward it, when I got near the car, if you have smelled that odor before, it was pretty clear." **– Sergeant John Allen**

"So in that moment in time you knew you had a murder on your hands?" **– Robyn Walensky**

"Well, I wouldn't say at that point we knew we had a murder but the facts were pretty clear. These facts were clear. We had a child that was missing, that had not been seen in a month, that car smelled like it had a dead body in it. We didn't really have anybody else missing. So, at that point, it was clear to us that that was certainly a possibility."

– Sergeant John Allen

"In regards to did I smell it myself? Yes, I did, and there is no question, working homicide for several years and being in the area of a bunch of decomposing bodies, that was the smell of a decomposing body. There's no question in my mind. That's what it was. There's no question if we were to open that can that's what I would smell again. I do know at the beginning there was a concern on how to keep that smell, make it tangible. Because I could talk about it, but unless there's something tangible to prove it, there's no way I can present it to someone else. I could simply say it smells like decomp so I actually had a friend who's a firefighter, he's a hazmat technician. And he's the one who mentioned the gas chromatograph mass spectrometry and he's the one who stated, 'Hey, if there's a smell in the air, it's caused by something. Let's find something to detect that smell.' And that's what led to the whole air sample thing."   **– Corporal Yuri Melich**

"Investigator Bloise and I started to work on the vehicle after midnight the night the car came in. It would be months before the car would leave the garage bay. When it first arrived, it was still a missing person's investigation. After the unmistakable odor was noted, the investigation took a different turn and the slow and methodical work began. Keep in mind there was no 'crime scene' located at the time; therefore, EVERYTHING we had, was in that car."
– Crime Scene Supervisor Michael Vincent

"I had a front-row seat to the entire trial. Every day I'd come to court and see all the evidence sitting in the center of the courtroom. The gas cans, items in large and small cardboard boxes all taped up, manila envelopes, large posters, color pictures, and then there were the canisters. I always wondered if the day would come when the canisters would be opened and the jurors would finally get to smell the 'whiff of death.' It never happened. Judge Perry ruled he didn't want the jurors to become 'witnesses' in the case. Yet the jurors were allowed to smell the Velveeta cheese wrapper."   **– Robyn Walensky**

"The Velveeta cheese wrapper was completely, completely empty, no food, nothing. I don't know why they tried to make that an issue because there never was cheese there. Everything was empty. I remember when defense attorney Jose Baez said 'garbage' and I said 'trash' and he said 'garbage' and I said 'trash.' Trash is something that is organic and garbage is something which is inorganic. So I explained that."
– CSI Geraldo Bloise

"One of the important things I want to talk about is that everyone talks about the smell of this car. She (Casey) threw the garbage in the trunk of her car, and like many of us, forgot sandwiches, leftovers, and doggie bags, she forgot to throw out the trash. This is the same day that she actually runs out of gas. That's where the smell comes from. This is the garbage from the trunk of the car."
– Jose Baez

"Baez has a big picture of the trash, he walks back and forth in the courtroom showing it to the jurors."
– Robyn Walensky

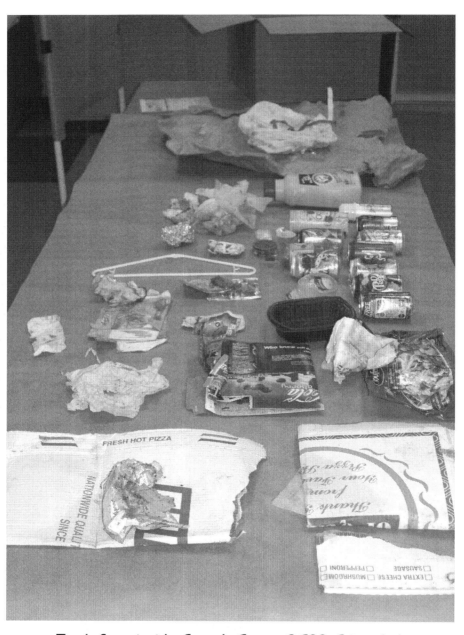

Trash from inside Casey's Car at OCSO Crime Lab
"Florida State Attorney's Office, 9th Judicial Circuit"

"It's wet, sticky. And what do the police do when they are done with it? They take it into an air room and they dry it out, so it can't, and you will see that once it dries out the smell goes away. And there's absolutely nothing that can be done to, to independently test or verify anything from this garbage. It's destroyed evidence. It's intentionally aired out."
– Jose Baez

"At trial, Jose Baez questions Geraldo Bloise about why he dried out the garbage found in the bag in Casey's car. It included thirty-seven items including the empty packages of pizza, lunch meat, and cheese along with other tossed items like empty soda cans. Bloise testifies he was following protocol, since drying out evidence preserves it and makes it easier to examine. The bag of garbage is critical, as Baez will continue to claim the foul odor in the car came from these discarded items. Prosecutors maintain the smell was coming from a decomposing body. Caylee's decomposing body."
– Robyn Walensky

"As hard as it is to accept, when Casey Anthony was at Blockbuster on June 16, walking arm in arm with her boyfriend Tony, Caylee was in the trunk of her car in the early stages of decomposition."
– Prosecutor Jeff Ashton during closing argument

"And now there is new science to actually test the air in the trunk."
– Robyn Walensky

CHAPTER 3

CANISTERS OF DEATH

"When you first opened it? What was your reaction?"
**– Prosecutor Jeff Ashton asking Dr. Arpad Vass,
Oak Ridge National Laboratory, about the canister
containing the carpet sample from Casey's car**

"I essentially jumped back a foot or two."
– Dr. Arpad Vass, Oak Ridge National Laboratory

"And did you immediately recognize the odor that was emanating from the piece of carpet in the can?" **– Prosecutor Jeff Ashton**

"Yes."
– Dr. Arpad Vass

"And what did you recognize that odor to be?" **– Jeff Ashton**

"I would recognize it as human decomposition odor."
– Dr. Arpad Vass

"That you smelled many, many times before?" **– Jeff Ashton**

"Twenty years' worth."
– Dr. Arpad Vass

"Dr. Arpad Vass is a senior research scientist and forensic anthropologist based at Oak Ridge National Laboratory in Oak Ridge, Tennessee. Vass has pioneered a technique that uses air samples to test for human decomposition. His experiments are aimed at determining how long a body has been deceased, or what he terms the 'post-mortem interval.' Dr. Vass works at a facility commonly known as 'the body farm,' located in Knoxville, Tennessee. To the average person it no doubt sounds like a spooky place or somewhere you'd visit on Halloween. At the body farm Dr. Vass and other scientists study bodies donated to science at various levels of decomposition. Over one thousand human bodies have been donated to date. They are left outside under various conditions. Some of the bodies are buried in the soil, others under a tarp, others are exposed to water, conditions in the woods, and some are studied as they deteriorate in the trunk of a car. Dr. Vass analyzes the chemicals as the body breaks down to determine time of death. He also studies clandestine graves. A number of bodies are buried at various depths. A piping system is installed at various levels. He monitors which chemicals are produced, either at the sight of the body or which chemicals seep upward in the soil columns, and he records all of the detailed data. Vass has a distinct speech impediment (for example: the word 'rapidly' he pronounces 'wapidly,' the word 'correct' he pronounces 'cowecht.' On the stand, Vass seems like a friendly, likeable scientist who speaks with enormous enthusiasm about his cutting-edge projects. He's so engrossed in his subject matter he starts talking technical and fast and he's losing his audience. The jurors are not taking notes and he's asked by the court reporter, and then in a lighthearted way by Prosecutor Jeff Ashton, to slow down."

– Robyn Walensky

"I love my subject."
– Dr. Arpad Vass says with a smile while testifying on the stand

"I can tell."
– Jeff Ashton laughs

"Dr. Vass continues. It's the breakfast hour and some of his testimony is gruesome. He talks about how the body liquefies during decomposition. He talks about the chemical vapors present at various stages of human decomposition. Dr. Vass attempts to slow it down and break it down for jurors. His research and his conclusions are detailed and thorough. The tests Dr. Vass has conducted and the conclusions he's reached have never been admitted in a trial in the United States, until today, June 6, 2011, and I have a front-row seat." **– Robyn Walensky**

"I collected the air samples. Dr Vass provided the equipment. I was the person to first contact each of the experts and ask for their assistance. So that made me the contact/go-between person for Dr. Vass, Dr. Haskell, and Dr. Hall. Dr. Vass shipped the necessary equipment, a portable air pump and test tube that contained three different types of filters. The filters are 'triple sorbent traps.' Dr. Vass also sent along specific instructions on how to operate the equipment, how long to run each test, and which areas he wanted me to test. The air in the garage, trunk, passenger area of the vehicle, and the trash. Five samples from the trunk liner were collected at the same time and placed in separate canisters. Two went to Dr. Vass, one went to the FBI, and two stayed in storage as backup in case another sample was needed for another type of test." **– Crime Scene Supervisor Michael Vincen**t

"I wonder if the CSIs doing this detailed work in that moment in time realize how the results may play out down the road in court."
– Robyn Walensky

"This science has never been admitted before a court of law. At the time, I knew it was going to be important. 'How important?' —Yes, I did realize it would be critical, as it was going to the first case in United States history that this was accepted in a court of law, so I proceeded according to Dr. Vass's specific instructions. The entire pump and the trap were placed in the trunk of the car and closed. The test was conducted for approximately seventy minutes. Then, I went into the interior of the vehicle, the passenger compartment. I also tested the air that was in our garage. The fourth air sample I did on the trash that was left inside the car. Each trap I secured in a vial and then I shipped them all back to Dr. Vass at the Oakridge lab."
– Crime Scene Supervisor Michael Vincent

"The car, as I told you, this car will be the subject of much debate. And you will hear evidence in this case that has never been admitted in a court of law, throughout the United States. The air samples that Ms. Drane Burdick told you about."

– Jose Baez

"Prosecutor Jeff Ashton continues and Dr. Vass testifies about the air samples and the extremely high levels of chloroform in Casey's trunk. Dr. Vass says the gases being emitted were consistent with a dead body being on the carpet. He describes his reaction to a container of air generated by a piece of trunk carpet from the Pontiac. Dr. Vass explains the stain on the carpet contains acids generated by early stage human decomposition. Vass is a research scientist who's studied decomposing bodies for two decades. He tells jurors he's shocked to find ten thousand times the amount of potentially deadly chloroform than would normally be expected in human decomposition alone. I am totally tuned in. As I sit in WDBO's seat #1, I find myself leaning forward in my chair, listening intently to Dr. Vass as he describes on the stand the four stages of human decomposition: fresh, bloat, active decay, and dry stage. A little technical, and a lot morbid, but being an anatomist's daughter, and having covered dozens of crime scenes over the past twenty-plus years of reporting, I am totally riveted. Dr. Vass then hits the emotional chords. He testifies he literally jumped back a foot or two due to the extremely potent smell."

– Robyn Walensky

"The odor was extremely overwhelming and strong and I was shocked that that little itty bitty can could have that much odor associated with it."

– Dr. Arpad Vass

"Jeff Ashton asks Vass about the number of times he's smelled a dead body. From start to finish, meaning when fresh dead bodies come in until the time they are skeletons. Dr. Vass says he's smelled fifty individuals. He has also smelled decomp on dozens of other occasions."

– Robyn Walensky

"Have you found the odor of human decomp to be a unique odor?"
– Jeff Ashton

"Yes."
– Dr. Arpad Vass

"Dr. Vass also testifies he's smelled the smell of dead animals, deer, dogs, cats, pigs."
– Robyn Walensky

"Have you found the odor of decomp to be distinguishable from the odor of the animal decomp you've experienced?"
– Jeff Ashton

"Animals have a more muskier scent. Domesticated animals like a pig have a sweeter scent."
– Dr. Arpad Vass

"It is clear to me from my view in seat #1, Dr. Vass believes a human body was decomposing in the trunk of the white Pontiac Sunfire driven by Casey Anthony, based on the forensic evidence."
– Robyn Walensky

"The reason we progressed is because the chloroform was shockingly high, unusually high."
– Dr. Arpad Vass

"Dr Vass continues, but now the math gets massive. Numbers that are hard to quantify. Chloroform can be a by-product of decomposition. Vass says normally in human decomp he sees chloroform in parts per trillion, meaning in very small amounts. But the concentration here is in the parts per MILLION range, meaning the levels are off-the-chart higher."
– Robyn Walensky

"This air sample, as Ms. Drane Burdick told you about…Dr. Arpad Vass, a very interesting man. Again, throughout the United States this evidence has never been admitted in a court of law. And this is an experiment that he conducted. Nothing more. An experiment in which you'll see flaw after flaw after flaw. It's never been validated. It's never been independently tested. And he can't find a single person in the entire world that would agree with his theories. It's going to be long, drawn out, and boring. But the fact of the matter is that they are getting desperate. Air samples, pure desperation. You'll hear that this scientist is somewhat of an inventor. In fact, what he's doing is, he invented a sniffer machine. Looks like a metal detector, so that he can sell it to law enforcement agencies across the country. And what he's using to determine the chemical composition of...of human decomposition is this database. Well, it's now being validated in this courtroom and he holds a patent to that machine and he stands to make millions, millions, and has an inherent bias by his testimony. You'll also hear that he has some other great ideas, like putting electronic leashes on flies to find dead bodies, and he also claims to be able to find hidden graves with a coat hanger. He's an interesting individual. And you'll get to hear plenty of his testimony, and it will be highly debated."

– Jose Baez

"We were shocked. We've never seen chloroform in those levels before, at least I haven't. The chloroform was shockingly high, unusually high."

– Dr. Arpad Vass

"So here are the takeaway points: A) Dr. Vass testifies the levels of chloroform in the can holding the carpet samples taken from the trunk were 'shockingly' high. B) Dr. Vass has never seen that high a level of chloroform in any sample ever sent to him for analysis. C) Dr. Vass tells jurors he's shocked to find ten thousand times (that's TEN thousand times, folks) the amount of potentially deadly chloroform than would normally be expected in human decomposition alone. Bottom line: I am not a scientist. But the raw science and test results are overwhelming. I am absolutely convinced a human body WAS decomposing in the trunk of Casey Anthony's car."

– Robyn Walensky

CHAPTER 4

DOGS DON'T LIE

"The nose knows. Another overwhelming piece of evidence, which will be ignored by jurors, is the two dogs that hit in the Anthony backyard and on Casey's car. Dogs don't lie."   **– Robyn Walensky**

"He gave a final trained alert in the southeast corner of the yard. There was a playhouse in the area," **– Deputy Jason Forgey testifies about his cadaver dog, "Gerus"**

"On Thursday, July 17, the Orange County Sheriff's Office had one of their cadaver dogs, which you will hear during the course of this trial is a dog that is specially trained in detecting the scent of human remains, do a sweep around the car. Deputy Jason Forgey, who has many of years of experience in handling police canines, and who has worked with his dog Gerus, prior to Gerus's recent retirement, took the dog around the car, at which point Gerus alerted, gave a trained final alert, which will be explained to you, on the trunk of the car, as having the odor of human remains."
     – Prosecutor Linda Drane Burdick during opening argument

"The trunk was open, Gerus jumped up into the trunk. Of course, I was overwhelmed at that point because I'm hitting at same time as he is."

– Deputy Jason Forgey

"You're gonna hear from a dog. While the dog can't get up there and testify, his handler is gonna talk about the dog and what he, what his dog allegedly said or reacted, or alerted to. And we're going to get into that when we talk about the forensics."
– Jose Baez during his opening argument

"Later that day, Gerus was taken to the Anthony residence, where again, George and Cindy Anthony had given permission to members of the Orange County Sheriff's Office to look in their yard, to see if there was any evidence that would help them learn what happened to Caylee, where was Caylee. And again in the backyard, near Caylee's playhouse, Gerus alerted to the odor of human decomposition."
– Prosecutor Linda Drane Burdick during opening argument

"Gerus alerts on two different locations in the backyard. One of the locations, Caylee's playhouse. The gift given to her by Cindy and George when she turns two. George assembles it and Caylee even has her own mailbox. Prosecutors believe Casey might have tried to bury Caylee's body here, but it is too difficult for her to dig up enough dirt."
– Robyn Walensky

"Deputy Forgey had asked that another canine handler, this one from the Osceola County Sherriff's Office, Kristin Brewer, Sergeant Brewer, brought her own canine cadaver dog to the Anthony home. And her cadaver dog also alerted to the odor of human decomposition in the playhouse in the Anthony's backyard. Now you will hear that crime scene technicians dug up in the areas where the dogs alerted, did not find Caylee."
– Prosecutor Linda Drane Burdick during her opening argument

"Based upon the dog alerts in the backyard, she (Casey) in all likelihood actually took Caylee's body back to the backyard and set it down for a period of time."
– Prosecutor Jeff Ashton during his closing argument

"Bones, the second cadaver dog, is brought in from a neighboring county. Bones's handler testifies to his record. She says on one occasion Bones was brought to a landfill for a search and he kept hitting on a blanket. No one could understand it. But after further investigation, it turns out a baby had been born on that blanket. Bones is just like Gerus. In their own special way, these dogs speak volumes." **– Robyn Walensky**

"Bones gave a 'trained final alert.'"
**– Sergeant Kristin Brewer, who handles K-9 "Bones,"
testifying as a prosecution witness**

"Sergeant Brewer tells the court Bones hits within feet of where Deputy Forgey's dog hit earlier in the vicinity of Caylee's playhouse. Jose Baez cross-examines Brewer about her search in the backyard. Baez making the point that just because a dog alerts on something, it doesn't mean Caylee's dead body was in the area."
– Robyn Walensky

"Such dogs are more of a tool than a conclusive indicator of human decomposition, especially when you don't have a body." **– Jose Baez**

"So while dogs can't talk, the evidence speaks volumes. If you play connect the dots, and apply logical thinking, the dogs tell us Caylee's body was A) in Casey's car and B) in the backyard. So in a nutshell, Casey most likely drove around for days with Caylee's body in the trunk. This is the prosecution's theory and it's backed by scientific evidence, plus the alerts of two highly trained cadaver dogs. When deputies are on scene at the Anthony home, George directs them to an area where he notices fresh dirt. Back on June 18, two days after Caylee goes missing, Casey borrows a shovel from a neighbor for about an hour. One and one equals two." **– Robyn Walensky**

"Cadaver dogs just don't lie. He did his job. I testified to everything that we did."
– Deputy Jason Forgey in interview with Robyn Walensky

CHAPTER 5

CSI: THIS IS NOT A TV SHOW

"As I sit in this cathedral of a courtroom at the top of the Orange County Courthouse; soaring ceiling, large windows and a balcony with rows of extra movie theater-style seating, I listen to conflicting testimony from various witnesses. I remind myself I am not watching CSI, the TV show. The science does not all add up neat and clean in under an hour, there's no music and quick fade to a commercial. Take for example: Casey's clothes. On August 6, 2008, a search warrant is issued and CSI Geraldo Bloise goes to the Anthony home to examine the clothes in her closet for stains. Bloise testifies at trial that no stains are found on the pants Casey wore on June 16, 2008, the day Caylee is last seen. On cross-examination, Bloise testifies Casey's mother, Cindy, admits she had washed those pants. On CSI, the TV show, there would be some sort of stain on the clothes that would instantly lead the TV detectives straight to the crime scene. But no such luck here. This is raw, unedited reality theater, and in real life, the evidence doesn't always line up neat and tidy like it does on TV in under an hour. This is heavy stuff. However, there are a few light moments, very few. The one that instantly comes to mind; Jose Baez sparking a huge outburst of laughter in the courtroom when he asks CSI Bloise about whether he talks while processing evidence."

– Robyn Walensky

"Do you speak while you're doing this?"　　　　　**– Jose Baez**

"No."　　　　　**– CSI Geraldo Bloise**

"Why not?"
– Jose Baez

"Because I'm by myself."
**– CSI Geraldo Bloise answers honestly and everyone laughs out
loud**

"But 99-percent of the time I spend in seat #1, during the morning session, absolutely no one is laughing, no one is even cracking a
smile. The reporters might say a friendly hello to each other, before
court starts, but that's it. Some of the spectators act like they just got
a ticket to a Broadway play. You can see how excited they are when
they spot the Anthony's sitting in court, or when Casey walks in, it's
as if they are spotting their favorite actor. Some seem star-struck. I
turn around from my front row seat and watch them, watch the key
players. Then they quickly settle into their seats, no snacks of course,
no bucket of popcorn, no gum chewing either. The Sheriff's deputies
warn the courtroom spectators they can't eat, fall asleep, or make
gestures. Only reporters who have a court issued credential are allowed to use their phones for texting and their iPads for tweeting.
Along with my Blackberry, I always bring with me a good ol' fash-
ioned large white legal pad on a clip board and a color magic marker
to make bold notes I can easily read. This way I can run outside and
do a live report from the bullet points I jot down in court. I try to
live by the Journalism 101 rule; "K.I.S.S." "Keep It Simple Stupid." If
I don't understand it, the audience won't understand it. I only get 30
seconds or so to tell the story, so the radio audience is getting bullet
points, highlights, or what I have always called "news nuggets." At
the beginning and end of the day, the Casey Anthony trial is a compli-
cated circumstantial case, with tons of forensic evidence. Some of it
yields excellent results, some does not. Take for example the shovel."
– Robyn Walensky

"Casey goes to the next-door neighbor and borrows a shovel. And I
would submit to you that the reason to borrow a shovel under those
circumstances is because she thought briefly about burying Caylee
in the backyard just like they buried their pets. Apparently, that was

too much work for her so she decided instead to just throw her in a swamp." **– Prosecutor Jeff Ashton during his closing argument**
"Casey backs her car into the Anthony family garage and borrows a shovel from neighbor Brian Burner just two days after Caylee is last seen. The FBI's Heather Seubert, a forensic DNA examiner, testifies there's an indication of 'possible female DNA' on the shovel but the amount is so small she could not draw scientific conclusions from it. On an episode of CSI, there would absolutely be a speck of dirt or DNA that would again lead the TV detectives straight to the victim, or as Gary Sinise, Detective Mac Taylor, most famously says on CSI New York 'the vic.'" **– Robyn Walensky**

"This is a dry-bones case. Very, very difficult to prove. The delay in recovering little Caylee's remains worked to our considerable disadvantage."
– Florida State Attorney Lawson Lamar during post-verdict news conference, July 5, 2011

"In almost every episode of CSI there is a blood stain, or blood spatter. This is what viewers are used to seeing on the tube. This is what jurors have come to expect at trial. But Lawson Lamar makes an excellent point about this being a "dry-bones case." It's a harsh reality, but there is no blood found. Not one blood drop. No blood - at all. The defense calls Heather Seubert, who in 2008, was a forensic supervisor of the DNA unit at the FBI lab in Quantico, VA. She is an expert in DNA and Serology, the scientific study of blood serum and other bodily fluids. On July 24, 2009, she receives Q-89, Caylee's shorts. No blood or semen is found on the shorts. She also examines Q-81, pieces of Caylee's 'Big Trouble Comes in Small Packages' T-shirt. Again, no blood on that item either." **– Robyn Walensky**

Pink T-shirt "Big Trouble Comes In Small Packages" (new)
"Florida State Attorney's Office, 9th Judicial Circuit"

Tattered letters from T-shirt "Big Trouble Comes In Small
Packages" found with Caylee's remains
"Florida State Attorney's Office, 9th Judicial Circuit"

Casey & Caylee (wearing the plaid shorts found with her remains)
"Florida State Attorney's Office, 9th Judicial Circuit"

Tattered pair of plaid shorts found with Caylee's remains
"Florida State Attorney's Office, 9th Judicial Circuit"

"Was there any blood on any of the clothing that you received from the Anthony home?"   **– Jose Baez**

"No sir, not on those items."   **– Heather Seubert, FBI DNA expert**

"Seubert testifies she tests for blood, semen, and other bodily fluids on multiple items. Nothing is found in Casey's car, on the car seat in the vehicle, on the steering wheel cover, on Casey's clothing, or with Caylee's remains. Prosecutor Jeff Ashton asks Seubert about the lack of blood evidence in all of her tests. Ashton asks if the absence of blood could be because the method of killing someone would produce no blood evidence, and Seubert agrees. So the bottom line here is, if Caylee died from a chloroform overdose, and then was suffocated with the duct tape and triple bagged, there would be no blood evidence."   **– Robyn Walensky**

CHAPTER 6

TOSSED LIKE TRASH

"They did show some pictures that will stay with me for life."
**– Juror 11, foreman, physical education teacher in his thirties,
in an exclusive interview with Fox's Greta Van Susteren, On the
Record**

"With regret I am here to inform you that the skeletal remains found on December 11 are those of the missing toddler Caylee Anthony. As our usual protocol, the next of kin has been notified prior to making this information public. This identification was made by nuclear DNA taken from a portion of the remains and compared to a known profile of Caylee Anthony. The DNA analysis was performed by the FBI lab in Quantico, Virginia."
**– Dr. Jan Garavaglia, Orange County chief medical examiner, at
a news conference on December 19 announcing the remains found
December 11 near the Anthony home are Caylee Anthony**

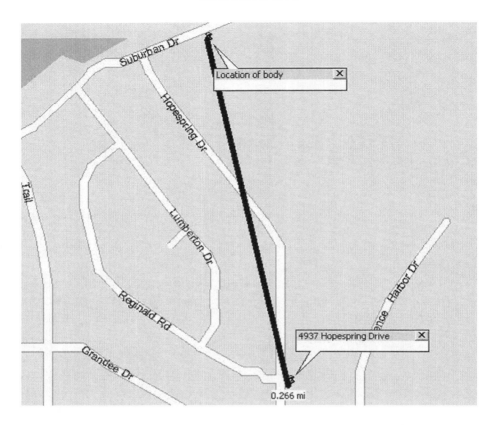

Map showing distance between Anthony Home & Woods Scene
"Florida State Attorney's Office, 9th Judicial Circuit"

Google Earth Map of Anthony Home & Woods Scene
"Florida State Attorney's Office, 9th Judicial Circuit"

"One of the first places I visit when I move to Orlando is the Anthony home and the woods where Caylee's remains are recovered. My immediate thought is, while I am not an Olympic athlete, I could easily walk here from the house, and drive here in literally a minute. Two minutes, tops. For three nights in a row, I do live reports from the swamp scene for HLN's Nancy Grace show."   **– Robyn Walensky**

Robyn Walensky reporting for HLN "Nancy Grace Show"
Photo Courtesy: Kristine & Wayne Stevens

"Nancy, I want to show you just how terrible this scene is. Walk with me if you will into the mud. I have boots on; you can hear, actually hear the sloshing. Whoever left this child here, whoever dumped this body in this scene never wanted little Caylee to be found again. It's so horrible out here, so hot, so buggy, so smelly."
                    – Robyn Walensky, HLN's Nancy Grace, July 18, 2011

"The remains are completely skeletonized with no soft tissue present."
                                            – Dr. Jan Garavaglia

"CSIs work around the clock, sifting through the woods scene, looking for bone fragments and any additional evidence. When they are done, the woods scene is completely stripped down as if a nuke hit it. No trees, no brush, no vines, the area completely bare. At every stage it is photographed."   **– Robyn Walensky**

"I know throughout the entire investigation, not just out at the actual scene, but at the entire investigation, I took over two thousand pictures, so it was a new experience. I've never worked on a crime scene over such a long period and so it was different."
                                            – CSI Jennifer Welch

"When I arrive at the location, I see a lot of personnel digging through the wooded area. I observe them removing human bones within the soil. The skull with the hair had already been transported to the morgue along with what remained of the skeleton. There are still bones being found that day, two days later, three days later. The center of the scene is approximately twenty feet in from the curb, down that hill. The entire area is covered over by vegetation. It's a heavily vegetated area with loads of bugs, trash, and junk. Basically a dump site. After the victim is located, it's verified by the first-responding deputy who notifies the proper personnel; detectives and the crime scene unit respond. The scene is expanded, the perimeter is expanded then the processing begins. First thing is to photograph the scene as it is, taking the amount of photographs necessary, a 360-degree view of the scene. But as many pictures as necessary. Then the area is

searched. Evidence is marked, and photographs are taken again. This scene is processed over the period of about ten days."
– Crime Scene Supervisor Michael Vincent

Woods before OCSO Crime Scene Detectives process the scene

Photo Courtesy: Orange County Sheriff's Office Forensics Unit

"I've been here at the Orange County Sheriff's Office now for thirty years. I've been to many crime scenes. I don't recall ever being at a scene that was worked by the forensics people as thoroughly as this was worked." **– Sergeant John Allen**

Woods after OCSO Crime Scene Detectives finish processing the scene

Photo Courtesy: Orange County Sheriff's Office Forensics Unit

"Adding to the cost of the investigation, both monetary and physical, several CSIs were making routine trips to the twenty-four-hour "Centra Care" doctors for medical attention from an array of harm endured from the nine-day stint in the heavily wooded lot. One CSI was pregnant, and on her hands and knees searching for the bones of a baby. At least two CSIs were bitten by spiders, and several CSIs had poison ivy. Mine so bad, my arms were covered in blisters which swelled and filled with liquid so that I couldn't even pull my sleeves up or turn my arms for fear of breaking skin. I had blisters in my ears and beneath my eyes from wiping away dirt and sweat. My doctor ordered me to not return to work, which I promptly ignored. Ultimately I ended up in the emergency room for full body hives as a reaction. The poison ivy scarred my arms for a solid year before the marks began to fade." **– CSI Alina Burroughs**

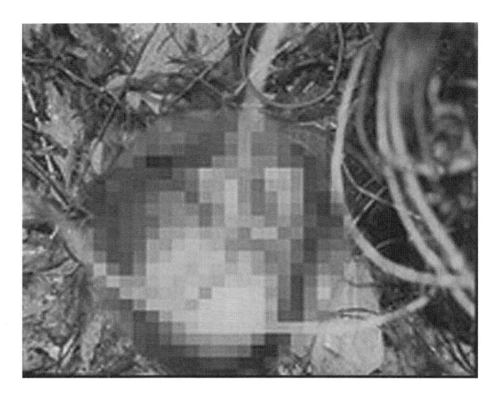

Caylee's Skull found in woods scene – modified for release to public
"Florida State Attorney's Office, 9th Judicial Circuit"

"Will the pictures of little Caylee's skull always stick with you for the rest of your career?"
– Robyn Walensky in an interview with CSI Jennifer Welch

"There are a lot of cases that I work that you always end up having in the back of your head, so, yes, this case probably will stick with me."
– CSI Jennifer Welch

"I mean, in a frightening sense?"   **– Robyn Walensky**

"No, not in a frightening sense. It will just be something that I'll remember and it will continue to remind me what I work for, which is finding justice for victims."   **– CSI Jennifer Welch**

"The manner of death though is an opinion based on available information, including examination of the body, information from the scene, as well as circumstantial evidence based on all of this, the manner of death in this case is homicide. The cause of death will be listed as homicide by undermined means." **– Dr. Jan Garavaglia**

"On the day that Dr. G made the announcement that the remains were, in fact, Caylee's, we gathered inside the mobile command post—standing room only—FDLE, FBI, sworn officers, and CSI... and when the words were said—even though we knew it was her. Each of us began to cry. We then returned to the scene, arms around shoulders in comfort—to continue to search for additional evidence."
– CSI Alina Burroughs

"The body of Caylee Anthony had been wrapped into a Winnie the Pooh blanket, stuffed into many garbage bags, thrown into a littered swamp like she was just another piece of trash. All that remained were scattered bones, remnants of clothes that she was wearing, and pieces of the plastic bag that had entombed her. Caylee spent many months in that swamp, roots encircled the blanket, they encircled her hair, they wrapped themselves into the bags that she was in. Duct tape covered the nose and mouth area of that tiny human skull. The duct tape was stuck in the hair, indicating that Caylee's killer never intended that it be removed."
– Prosecutor Linda Drane Burdick during her opening argument

"As heartless as the killer is, I see evidence of a woman's touch. Someone placed a heart-shaped sticker on the duct tape directly over Caylee's mouth as if to say, 'I love you.' The heart-shaped sticker leads detectives to one place, Casey Anthony's bedroom."
– Robyn Walensky

CHAPTER 7

HEART-SHAPED STICKERS

"We were finishing up at the scene. It was our final day—the search was over. I was approached by my supervisor and a handful of detectives saying that we had a warrant to conduct at the (Anthony) house. CSIs packed up their vans and hurriedly put away sifters and buckets, which were coated in dirt. Helicopters hovered overhead and we made plans to drive out together—each Investigator taking a different path as not to draw attention to the Anthony house and the few vans that went toward it instead of away. We passed a crowd of cheering citizens; as each van rolled past, they clapped and yelled as a sign of their support. We descended on the house and decided on a plan for searching, photographing, documenting, and collecting evidence. The first room we went to was Casey's. Binders, folders, and boxes were opened and flipped through—when I saw the heart-shaped stickers, my first thought was damn, these aren't an exact match. My second thought was...who keeps this many heart-shaped stickers in their house? I am a woman, and I don't have heart-shaped stickers in my house. Yes, walls of her room were full of artwork—photograph collages of her...and photograph collages of Caylee. No finger paint, no macaroni glued to paper, nothing adorned with heart-shaped stickers. Nothing. My mind flashed to a time when Casey was out of jail—ornamented with her "help find Caylee" shirt she jumps into the passenger seat of an SUV with white paint on the back...Caylee's name and a hand-drawn white heart."
– CSI Alina Burroughs

"There's a multitude of evidence surrounding heart-shaped Stickers. As a crime reporter, this is the kind of evidence that catches my ear early on in this mystery and I zero in on it. It reminds me of the DC sniper case back in 2002. The killers, John Allen Muhammad and Lee Boyd Malvo, would leave a tarot card, their "calling card" at some of their bloody crime scenes. I remember watching Montgomery County Police chief Charles Moose discussing it on TV as the tarot card nugget was leaked by a detective to a reporter. It was critical evidence Moose did not want released. As a crime reporter, the tarot card totally piques my interest when I hear about it for the first time; equally, so do the heart-shaped stickers in the Caylee Anthony case. There are three pieces of evidence pertaining to the stickers. The first is the piece of cardboard with a heart-shaped sticker on it found in the vicinity of Caylee's remains in the woods. Second, there is evidence about an outline of a heart-shaped sticker observed on the duct tape found over Caylee's mouth while the FBI examiner looks at it under ultraviolet light. Third, sheets of heart-shaped stickers are found by CSI Alina Burroughs inside the Anthony home, in Casey's bedroom."
– Robyn Walensky

"The heart-shaped stickers were outlined in the warrant, so I knew what we were looking for when we left the crime scene. As far as when we found them, I know it was the first room we went to, so it was within twenty minutes of getting to the house. There was a folder with red heart-shaped stickers missing three stickers and a binder with a sheet of multicolored heart-shaped stickers cut in half in the binder. The sticker backing (no sticker) was in the box with the baby shower items. All of which were in the dresser in Casey's bedroom."
– CSI Alina Burroughs

"The FBI cannot link these sheets of stickers collected in Casey's bedroom to the one on the cardboard at the crime scene, as it's raised. The sheets of heart-shaped stickers from the bedroom are flat."
– Robyn Walensky

"During my examination of Q63, an outline of a heart appeared on one of the corners and an edge of that piece of duct tape. It was approximately the size of a dime."

– Elizabeth Fontaine, forensic examiner, FBI Latent Print Unit

"At trial, the technician from the FBI testifies there is an imprint. She notices something unusual, the outline of a heart on one of the three pieces of duct tape tagged item Q63 while examining it under special lighting known as RUVIS—Reflected Ultra-Violet Imaging System. What she sees is adhesive from a heart-shaped sticker on the duct tape covering the mouth of Caylee's remains. She testifies that she makes a note of the imprint, but admits she never took a picture of it. A scientist with absolutely no common sense. How can she not snap a photograph of this?"

– Robyn Walensky

"If you were to wear a Band-Aid for an extended period of time and you remove that Band-Aid, you have the glue residue outlining the surface. The outline of the heart resembled that. Instead of being in the shape of a Band-Aid, it was in the shape of a heart."

– Elizabeth Fontaine

"An FBI supervisor also sees the heart shape, but when Fontaine attempts to photograph it later it's no longer visible because of the other forensic tests which have been performed, including one with colored dye. Questioning the evidence presented, lead defense attorney Jose Baez, during cross-examination, notes that when Fontaine examined the duct tape for a second time, the heart-shaped residue was gone and could no longer be seen. Fontaine also testifies that no fingerprints were detectable on the three pieces of duct tape analyzed with Caylee's remains, although this comes as no surprise, she says, because of the exposure to the environment and outside elements. Fontaine is asked three times if she's able to recover fingerprints on each piece of tape and three times she answers with the same exact sentence."

– Robyn Walensky

"No, I was not."

– Elizabeth Fontaine

"I also find in Casey's bedroom a keepsake box with baby shower items. In it is an envelope with sticker backing, but missing the actual heart-shaped sticker. Everything I collected relating to the stickers was in the dresser in Casey's room." **– CSI Alina Burroughs**

"I ask Alina about tests run on this multitude of stickers."
– Robyn Walensky

"No, nothing matched." **– CSI Alina Burroughs**

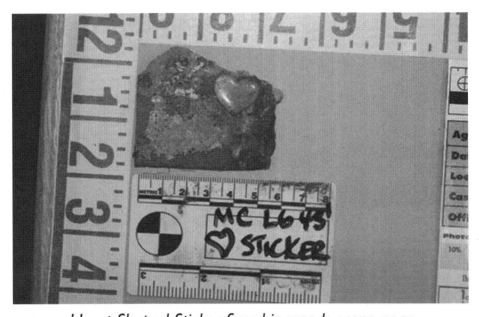

Heart Shaped Sticker found in woods scene near
Caylee's remains
"Florida State Attorney's Office, 9th Judicial Circuit"

CHAPTER 8

SOLO STRAND

"There's no fibers, there's no hair, there's no DNA, there's no finger-prints of Casey's or anyone in our family."
— **Cindy Anthony on NBC's TODAY Show, August 13, 2010**

"DNA became a household word during the OJ Simpson trial. It was new, and the only man who seemed to really understand the science in that Los Angeles courtroom was Barry Scheck, a key member of Simpson's 'Dream Team.' In the Casey Anthony Trial in 2011, we learn about 'post-mortem root banding.' The test can show if a hair is connected to a person who's alive or one who's dead."
— **Robyn Walensky**

"I found the hair. Q-12. This was the hair that came back positive with the DNA, the mitochondrial DNA from the mother. That hair, yes, I found it."
— **CSI Geraldo Bloise**

"FBI hair and fiber expert Stephen Shaw testifies the hair CSI Bloise finds in the trunk matches the hair found on Caylee's skull in the woods. The hair in the woods shows a later stage of decomposition."
— **Robyn Walensky**

"Oh, wow, it was amazing. I was busy checking the trunk, I was look-ing with my magnifier and I see a little red fiber over to the left side and I say, 'Wait a minute, this is a hair. 'I collected it immediately. It

was amazing. Yeah, it was amazing. When I received the results from the FBI lab, I said, 'Wow. That was the hair I collected with my hands.' I always say it was, 'divine intervention.' I feel that way."
– CSI Geraldo Bloise

"FBI analyst Karen Lowe testifies Q-12, the hair CSI Bloise finds in the trunk exhibits characteristics of "apparent decomposition" and specifically a post-mortem root banding. The FBI's Stephen Shaw does a study to determine if hairs take from a live person – subjected to all types of environments – develop the 'decomposition band' found on the trunk hair, Q-12. He testifies while he can't say with 100 percent certainty the Q-12 came from a dead body—in his experience he has never seen hair banding that did not come from a corpse."
– Robyn Walensky

"I'll always remember finding the hair. It's like looking for a needle in the stack. This is very hard to get a hair in that condition. I was alone when I found it, yes. I said look, why, when I saw the red fiber in the left corner inside the trunk, the hair was on top and then when I put my magnifier with my flashlight, I said, 'Wait a minute, this is a hair,' and I collected it. But, you know, I collected about several vacuums and I collected several hairs by hand but that particular hair was the only one that came positive with DNA from the mother, which is amazing. "I was completely shocked when I saw the results, it was amazing."
– CSI Geraldo Bloise

"Now, I want to touch briefly and I'm just about to wrap it up, on some of the forensics you'll hear throughout this case. You're gonna hear about the car evidence and a possible hair, one hair. What Ms. Drane Burdick didn't tell you is the FBI lab analyst was telling everyone and she'll probably come and tell you too, that she can't say for certain that that hair came from a dead body. In fact, she sent out a request asking to find more hairs. And they did. We hired Dr. Henry Lee, one of the world's greatest forensic scientists, to go in and, and search that car. And he found seventeen different hairs, seventeen more hairs. And before you start wondering what is Caylee's hair doing in there, in the trunk of the car—well, Casey's hair, other people's hair, was in the trunk of the car. We often shed hairs very easily. None of that, absolutely none of the other hairs, and I think there was a total of twenty-seven that ended up being inspected, had what they call the banding, the discoloration. This was a problem for them. So when we went and took the depositions of the analysts, they got a bright idea. They decided to conduct a study. After we took their deposition, they realized that they had something that was not validated. So, they did a study of live hairs in trunks, in water, exposed to all different elements. And they found a couple of—and they had a couple of what is called blind examinations that showed that there were some characteristics shown from live hairs. This is very questionable. And you will hear that it is rarely, if ever, done on one single hair, this type of analysis. Because you need more, you need to be able to be certain. And this hair means nothing."

– Jose Baez during his opening argument

"A single nine-inch-long brown hair found in the car trunk of accused child killer Casey Anthony could have been ripped from the dead body of her two-year-old daughter, an FBI expert testified on Saturday. Jose Baez contends the science behind some of the hair analysis is new and unreliable." **– Robyn Walensky**

"Well, they tested more hairs that they found. They did all kinds of tests. They all came back negative. Negative, negative, negative. The only thing that they are trying so desperately to tie Caylee to is the car. But one, if we get back to its basic—get back to the very basics here—is how did Caylee die? How did Caylee die? The car doesn't shed any light on that. At best, it tells you that she was transported."

– Jose Baez

"So here is the wrap-up: Stephen Shaw, a hair and fiber expert from the FBI, testifies a single hair strand found in the trunk of Casey's Pontiac revealed "post-mortem root banding," which he stated was unique to deceased individuals only. Dr. Arpad Vass, from Oak Ridge National Laboratory, concludes a decomposing body was in the trunk of Casey's car. Karen Lowe, who specializes in microscopic examination of hair samples at the FBI Laboratory in Quantico, Virginia,

testifies she found "root-banding" on the hair, something she says scientists have never seen other than on hairs from decomposing bodies.
"It has darkened bands at the root portion… this is consistent with
apparent decomposition. I made a determination that it was similar
to a hair in a hairbrush that was identified as belonging to Caylee
Anthony." Lowe says this was the first trial at which she has testified
about hair root banding. In previous cases involving hairs with root
banding, she said, the hairs came from known bodies and, therefore,
hair banding was not a critical issue. So the bottom line is this folks:
the nine-inch long hair did not belong to Casey or Cindy. Both wore
their hair short. The nine-inch hair was not dyed. Cindy colored her
hair blonde and Casey changed her hair color too. The strand found
in the trunk was hair discolored at the root in a way that matches a
decomposing human body. Period."

– Robyn Walensky

CHAPTER 9

FANTASY FORENSICS

"There are some key take away phrases at trial, 'I need you in my life,' the now infamous text George Anthony sent Krystal Holloway aka River Cruz. There's 'snowballed out of control.' But the big catch phrase is uttered by Jose Baez, "fantasy forensics." And just like Johnny Cochran famously said at OJ Simpson's Trial, 'If the gloves don't fit you must acquit.' Fantasy forensics" sticks and no doubt ticks off and insults some of the CSIs who've worked 24-7 for three years on this case." **– Robyn Walensky**

"We're not talking about fantasy forensics anymore."
– Jose Baez during his closing argument trying to discredit the science

"Didn't it piss you off when he's up there saying 'fantasy forensics' and 'junk science'? Didn't that piss you off?"
– Robyn Walensky in an interview with CSI Geraldo Bloise

"I'm telling you right now, I don't care what he said about the forensic fantasy. Every piece of evidence that I saw made it through the trial was good and admitted in the trial. That's it. That's it.

This is real forensic work. We are proud that we submitted the evidence to the FBI. All the results came back with good, positive results. For example, the hair—the decomposed hair—from the victim. So,

that was real forensic evidence that was submitted to the FBI. The air samples, the stain, the carpet, everything was real. Everything passed in the trial and everything was submitted in the court of law."
– CSI Geraldo Bloise, standing firmly by his technical work

"I ask CSI Jennifer Welch how she feels about Jose Baez using the phrases 'junk science' and 'fantasy forensics.'" **– Robyn Walensky**

"I was disappointed in hearing that. I think forensics speak the facts. Unlike suspects or witnesses who can tell a story; I think the evidence speaks for victims who no longer can." **– CSI Jennifer Welch**

"As for the forensics. Jose Baez has called the work "junk science," while Oak Ridge Labs calls Dr. Vass's work "groundbreaking science."
– Robyn Walensky

"I know Dr. Vass. I've become acquainted with him over the course of the investigation. I think the science he does is legitimate science. I think it's a phenomenal thing that he does. With the root banding, this is science advancing on itself. I can't explain or can't speak for what the jurors felt or what they took in or what they didn't take in. I don't know if they understood it. I don't know if they didn't understand it. I can't tell you. I can tell you I understood it and I think Dr. Vass has made great strides in our scientific community to prove a case." **– Corporal Yuri Melich**

"I can't say what the jurors thought. I thought with every little piece of evidence, I thought we had a very strong circumstantial case. Obviously the jury didn't see it that way. I thought the state did a great job presenting the evidence." **– Sergeant John Allen**

"Solid science is normally death to the defense team trying to protect the defendant from it. But as we see in the first OJ Simpson trial if the jurors don't understand the science, or don't want to believe the science, it's death to the prosecution's case." **– Robyn Walensky**

"Junk Science…They'll ask you to see things that aren't there, and they'll ask you to imagine fictional science, it's a fantasy of forensics…They couldn't find a single link from Casey to Caylee's death. Not a single link. That's what this case is about, an accident that snowballed out of control." **– Highlights of key phrases used by Jose Baez**

"Extremely strong words in the form of catchy phrases from the defense team. I'm instantly reminded of Johnnie Cochran at the OJ Simpson trial talking about the bloody glove, "If it doesn't fit you must acquit." I wonder how pissed off the CSIs are right now, hearing the words 'junk science' and 'fantasy forensics.'" **– Robyn Walensky**

"We have a protocol for that because basically at every single crime scene, if we have any items which are wet or moist, we have to dry them out. This is normal. For instance, when we have blood when it's fresh, we put it in the dry room, in a special dry room. This is normal. And in that way, the evidence never was altered. Baez can say what he wants, it was never altered." **– CSI Geraldo Bloise**

"No doctors or lawyers on the jury. One of the jurors, a retired woman in her sixties, was working at a Publix Supermarket. So when the scientific evidence starts to be introduced at trial, I really wonder if these folks will actually grasp the material." **– Robyn Walensky**

CHAPTER 10

DUCT TAPE = THE MURDER WEAPON

"Follow the tape." **– Jose Baez during opening statements**

"There is no question that that tape was on Caylee's face before her body decomposed because otherwise the mandible wouldn't have been in place and it was. You can see the photographs of the tape, the duct is curved slightly under the jaw, there are even strands of the duct tape that go under the jaw. That tape was placed there for one singular purpose. Now we can only hope that the chloroform was used before the tape was applied, so that Caylee went peacefully without fear...But go she did, and she died because she could not breathe. She died because she had three pieces of duct tape over her nose and mouth. And she died because her mother decided that the life that she wanted was more important. This murder was premeditated and the defendant is guilty."

– Prosecutor Jeff Ashton in closing argument

"Although no one knows for sure, the state maintains the duct tape was the murder weapon. I believe chloroform was also in play. Perhaps Caylee's heart stopped? No one knows. We do know duct tape was used by the killer and it was wrapped around Caylee's small skull."

– Robyn Walensky

"Let me echo the words of Dr. Jan Garavaglia, the medical examiner in this case. She said, 'There is no good reason to put duct tape over the face of a child.' Why would you put duct tape over the face of a child? There's two reasons, one is perhaps to silence them. But then why do you need three? Remember in this case there wasn't one piece of duct tape placed over Caylee's face; there were three, overlapping at angles, placed over her face. Why do you need three? What does three do, that one does not? One would certainly silence her, if for some reason that's what you wanted to do, as brutal as that would be. Why would you need three? You need three because your purpose is not to simply silence the child, your purpose is to make sure the child cannot breathe. The first piece goes over the mouth, that doesn't secure the nose, the second piece goes over the nose, but there's gaps so you have to be thorough; you have to have three, one, two, three, and then, the child dies. There is simply no other reason, there is no other justification, there is no common sense. There is just no reason to put duct tape over the face of a child living or dead. And that, ladies and gentlemen, is proof beyond a reasonable doubt of how Caylee died." **– Jeff Ashton during his closing argument**

"They checked the duct tape. The duct tape had no finger prints. They ran every kind of finger printing exam you can. No finger prints on the duct tape. One of the easiest ways of being able to, uh, lift finger prints is off duct tape. Yes, the duct tape was deteriorated to a certain extent but they still tried at the FBI. They, also, searched the duct tape for DNA. No DNA of either Casey or Caylee. But yet they want you to believe that she had duct tape wrapped around her mouth and was decomposing, completely decomposed and not a shred of DNA on her. …there was DNA on her. DNA from an FBI analyst. They contaminated the duct tape. DNA is so sensitive, so easily attachable that an analyst in the documents department contaminated the duct tape. And there's also another profile on there, who they don't know, a partial profile. Someone they don't know. But it's only at what they call one marker. So it's impossible to find who that DNA belongs to. But it is not impossible to exclude both Casey and Caylee, completely excluded. There's usually what we call thirteen different markers where they test DNA. Unfortunately this is one, only one.

Could be contamination, or could not be. But there's one thing for certain; there's no forensic evidence that ties Casey to this. Again, she's too stupid to—she's dumb enough to leave the body off the side of the road but yet smart enough to leave zero forensic evidence. Something's, something's not right here. Something doesn't make sense."

– Jose Baez

George Anthony's Red Gas Can with 'Henkel' Brand Duct Tape on it
"Florida State Attorney's Office, 9th Judicial Circuit"

"To further confuse and create reasonable doubt, the defense team links the all important duct tape to the state of Ohio, where the Anthony's used to live and to father George Anthony, and the duct tape on his gas cans. All we hear at trial is the duct tape came from Ohio. Father George lived in Ohio. The defense wants jurors to believe that since he and the duct tape came from Ohio—father George killed Caylee. It's an incredible leap. And it's flat-out absurd. But to his credit Jose Baez does a great job leading jurors down this path. In reality the duct tape was manufactured in North Carolina. It is a key piece of evidence; the murder weapon. Unfortunately the duct tape did not yield DNA. And unlike every episode of CSI, jurors didn't get to see a fingerprint on any of the duct tape." **– Robyn Walensky**

"On November 3, 2010, I flew to Charlotte, North Carolina, and drove to Stony Point to Shurtape Technologies. I was requested by my commanding officer to transport the duct tape to the factory where it was manufactured. The duct tape is not from Ohio. The duct tape was collected at the crime scene, and then packaged by the Medical Examiner's Office, and then sent to the FBI. The FBI sent the duct tape back to the Orange County Evidence Unit for storage. My supervisor in Orange County asked me specifically, 'Can you fly it up to the factory to be examined to see if it is their product and if it was manufactured by them?' I said yes. When I picked up the duct tape at the Orange County Evidence Unit, it was in a sealed manila enve-lope. When I opened the package, there was a clear envelope inside, and in it I could see the duct tape. It was grey or silver in color. The condition: dry rotted. To my eye, it had been under water for quite a while and then dried out and deteriorated. I knew this was one of the key pieces of evidence in the case. I was going to physically fly with it in my briefcase to another state. This piece of evidence was extreme-ly important. Where the company shipped this product to. How long it was made. Turns out the tape hadn't been manufactured for a few years. Two on-site technicians analyzed it. They looked at pieces of the duct tape I brought with me under the microscope while I stood by and observed. They said the duct tape had really deteriorated, but they came to the conclusion it was, in fact, their product. They showed me a sample of the stamp pattern and they tried to find a roll that matched it. But couldn't find the roll. But the bottom line is—it was theirs. I repackaged the evidence, drove it back to the airport, and flew back to Orlando with the results the same day. Because the duct tape was so weather beaten and deteriorated, there was no evi-dentiary value other than being duct tape placed on the child's face. There were no fingerprints, no DNA, no sticky surface; the sticky surface was totally gone, which would have held fibers, DNA, and fingerprints. It's a case-by-case basis when duct tape is under water how much it yields in information. In these kinds of weather conditions, for that length of time it yielded nothing. If there was any evidentiary value it was lost because of weather and time."

– Crime Scene Supervisor Michael Vincent

"Faced with overwhelming evidence that the story is a lie, Casey comes up with a new one. Call it 'Casey 3.0, a new version'…The tape that is found on Caylee Anthony's remains which is contained in this bag…three pieces of duct tape with a distinctive brand on it, Henkel brand duct tape found on Caylee's body. The difficulty for 'Caylee 3.0' is that the same tape that was found on Caylee's body is also found on a gas can taken from her home…This tape is a fairly rare type of tape, hasn't been sold since 2007, and even then only a couple hundred thousand rolls of it sold—very unusual tape—and it's on Caylee's body and it's on that exhibit. And, in fact, in what has got to be the most bizarre part of this case, that very tape was used unknowingly by her own father to display a photograph of Caylee, that missing person poster, the tape that was used to kill Caylee Anthony was used to implore people to look for her."

– Jeff Ashton during his closing argument

"Duct tape to me is used to seal something. To literally close a box or to shut someone up. During his closing argument, Jeff Ashton hits the nail on the head, delivering a powerful summation of why he thinks Caylee was silenced."

– Robyn Walensky

"But there is a problem. The only way Casey's lies work is if Caylee isn't talking. Caylee is two and a half, almost three. She's starting to become verbal she is starting to talk. Caylee is not going to cooperate. She can't; she doesn't know enough to lie. At some point Caylee is going to say something. Someone is going to ask her about Zanny and she's going to say, 'Who?' Someone is going to ask her, 'Did you have a good time at Zanny's?' and she's going to say, 'No, Tony.' It just can't keep going."

– Jeff Ashton

CHAPTER 11

A LITANY OF LIES

"Casey Anthony maintains her lies until they absolutely cannot be maintained anymore…"
– Prosecutor Jeff Ashton during closing argument

"My entire life has been taken from me, everything has been taken from me, you don't understand, everybody wants me to have answers, I don't have any answers because I don't know what's going on, I have no one to talk to."
– Casey Anthony whining in a jailhouse interview, speaking to parents Cindy and George Anthony, August 14, 2008

"She has more characters than Disney."
– Robyn Walensky in an on-air interview with WDBO Radio morning host Jim Turner

"There are some truly crazy people on the planet. But in all my years as a reporter covering crime stories I never heard anyone tell such elaborate lies. Casey Anthony lies about her pregnancy, she lies about the baby daddy. There is no father listed on Caylee's birth certificate. It's absolutely endless. But her lies will be known around the world. The events of June 16, and the fibs that follow will haunt the family forever. And the day goes like this: Her father George Anthony is the last to see Casey walk out the door with Caylee. The date is June 16, 2008. He will never see her alive again. For thirty-one days, Casey makes up a multitude of stories, telling her parents she's with

Caylee in Tampa, Jacksonville, with her fictitious babysitter, 'Zanny the nanny' aka Zenaida Fernandez-Gonzalez, at the beach or at an Orlando theme park. There's a car accident. Zanny is at the hospital. Delay, delay, delay. Lie, after lie, after lie. The truth is Casey is care-free, hanging out with the man in her life, her friends, and hitting the clubs, dancing the night away in downtown Orlando. I think the charade would have lasted longer, perhaps sixty-one days, ninety-one days, a hundred and one days. Casey never reported Caylee missing. She never told a soul. Her friends didn't have a clue. Had Cindy not called 9-1-1 after smelling the odor of death wafting from the trunk of her daughter's car, the fabrications would have absolutely contin-ued. Let's face it; here's a girl who told her parents for two years she had a job at Universal Studios yet not one day did she ever work there."

– Robyn Walensky

"In what can only be described as if it weren't true—you couldn't write it this good—is the incident at Universal Studios, but it's in-dicative of Casey Anthony, of who she is and what she does.

– Prosecutor Jeff Ashton

"I had no reason to dispute her credibility when I first got there. Obviously there were concerns that she may not be telling us the truth of the matter, but again, I'm walking into it, I don't know what she's told other people. It doesn't matter what she's told other peo-ple. What she tells me is going to be what I need to worry about. As detailed as she was with her statement, I had no reason to doubt it. It might not have seemed logical but I had no reason to doubt it. Why would she go through a four-page written statement? And I went over that four-page written statement. She didn't come across as a mother of a missing child that was really worried about her child's well-being. And I say that because she didn't show any emotion. She was talking to me just how you are to me now. Very, almost mono-tone, without emotion. Just, 'Yes, I was here. Yes, I dropped her off there.' There was no crying, there was no 'go find my baby.' You had more emotion from her grandmother, than you did from her."

– Corporal Yuri Melich

"At four in the morning on Wednesday July 16, Detective Yuri Melich of the Orange County Sheriff's Office first arrives at the Anthony house. He gets a copy, or he reviews that handwritten statement of Casey Anthony, and he asks to speak with her. She talks with him in a room in the house. He ultimately tape-records their conversation. And he says, 'Is this true? Do you want to change anything on this statement?' And Casey Anthony says no sir, no way, this is what happened, I'm telling you the truth. One of the things that she had relayed to the Orange County Sheriff's Office was that she had a phone, another phone that was lost at Universal Studios, where she worked, that there were people who were employees of Universal Studios who she had told about this situation. Detective Melich again asked Casey if she could take him to the location where she says she last saw her daughter at the Sawgrass Apartments, and she takes him right back to that same place where she took the patrol officers. He asks if there are other people related to this Zenaida Fernandez-Gonzales that he could contact in an effort to locate Caylee Anthony. She takes him to the area of another residence, supposedly of Zenaida Gonzales's mother. No one is contacted, nobody is found, they return to the Hopespring house with no Caylee. Casey Anthony goes back in her house, and Yuri Melich begins his investigation. And that investigation begins at Universal Studios. Yuri Melich contacts an employee of Universal Studios by the name of Leonard Turtora in an effort to determine where Casey Anthony works, where these other people that she said can be contacted work, how they can be contacted. And Detective Melich learns Casey Anthony doesn't work at Universal Studios. Casey Anthony hasn't worked at Universal Studios for years. These people that she told you were here, they don't work here.
So Detective Melich, with the assistance of his supervisor, John Allen, and another detective by the name of Appie Wells, made contact with Casey. The first contact is made by Detective Melich over the phone, where he calls Casey Anthony and says, you work at Universal Studios and this is the information? Verifying what she had told him before. She says absolutely, of course, yes, you're right, that's it. She knows it's a lie. Maybe they all have it wrong. Maybe if Casey comes out to Universal Studios we can clear this up. Maybe we didn't get the names right, maybe I wrote it down wrong. And she is contacted

and agrees to come out to Universal Studios. So Detective Melich is there with Leonard Turtora, and John Allen and Appie Wells go to the Anthony house and pick up Casey Anthony, and she accompanies them to Universal Studios." **– Linda Drane Burdick**

"First time I see her, she's at home and I asked her, 'We're here following up trying to find your daughter. Would you come with us to talk some more?' She agreed to go with us. And when I asked her in the car, 'Listen, we'd like to go by Universal and I understand you're an event planner out there. We'd like to go look around your office to see if there's any evidence that might help us find your child.' She agreed. She directed me where to drive. We pulled into the parking lot." **– Sergeant John Allen**

"In the car she just has some idle chitchat with them on the way, and they get to the security gate at Universal Studios. And she's denied access. They're suggesting she doesn't work here. They ask her for identification. She says I don't have it, I forgot it.

Leonard Turtora, who's there with Yuri Melich, allows them to come in anyway. And there Casey Anthony is supposed to show them the office where she works and where she lost her phone, and where there might be some information about Zenaida Gonzales. And you will hear testimony that Casey Anthony walks with purpose through that security gate, and heads towards an administration building, walks in, and…True to what we've seen, or what you will see during this case, she's at the end of the hall. And she puts her hands in her back pocket, and smiles. 'All right, I don't work here.' Detectives Allen, Wells, and Melich then speak with Casey Anthony in a conference room at Universal Studios where she admits to them, that she's been lying to them about working at Universal. Because that's the lie, the evidence will show, they caught her in. But she will not waver at that point from her story, about the nanny. So, in an effort to find this person she insists exists, the detectives take her from Universal and show her pictures in the driver's license database of individuals with the name Zenaida Gonzalez. She doesn't know any of them. None of these Zenaida Gonzalez's on your driver's license pictures are my

Zenaida Gonzalez. At this point, since Casey Anthony admitted to them that she lied during the process of this investigation, she was arrested. And at this point, the investigation by necessity takes two different paths. There's the investigation that continued in the attempt to locate this person that Casey Anthony insisted had her daughter, this Zenaida Gonzalez." **– Linda Drane Burdick**

"She was very nice. Very friendly. Very cordial. We made small talk on the way there. She pointed us into the employee lot. We actually walked with her up to the employee entrance. We stood there at the employee entrance and we watched her talking with the security guard, listening to her talk to the security guard, telling the security guard that she had an office in the HR building." **– Sergeant John Allen**

"I wonder if Casey thinks these detectives are idiots." **– Robyn Walensky**

"I can't say what she thought, but we stood there and watched this and the security guard was checking his roster of employees. And we watched the exchanges and the security guard says, 'I'm sorry, ma'am, nobody by that name works here. We knew she was lying. We knew this was all bogus. Of course we knew. Obviously, anytime someone takes you someplace and lies to you, that's a charade. We ultimately walked into the back parking lot and we walked up and we allowed her to take us where she obviously didn't work. We walked into the HR building and once we walked to a dead end hall, there's no place else to go, she finally turned and said, 'OK, I don't work here.' And at that point, we sat down and did the interview that's all taped." **– Sergeant John Allen**

"None of us are sitting here believing what you're saying because everything that's coming out of your mouth is a lie." **– Detective Yuri Melich to Casey Anthony**

"This is the honest to God's truth, I don't know where she is. The last person that I saw her with is Zenaida." **– Casey Anthony**

"Listen, we know that's not true. We already know that you're not telling us the truth. You know what happened to Caylee – and you know where Caylee is."
– Corporal Yuri Melich

"This goes on for a grueling forty minutes. Melich tries different approaches as he hits the brick wall. Melich alternates between being aggressive and then not so harsh as he tries to get Casey to reveal where Caylee is."
– Robyn Walensky

"I can look at you as a person who's scared, or we can look at you as cold, callous, and a monster who doesn't care. It's gonna be one of those two options."
– Corporal Yuri Melich to Casey Anthony during taped interview at Universal Studios

"You listen to Yuri Melich grilling Casey and you almost want to cheer. He probably is the first person in her life to verbally nail her to the wall and call her out on her lies. It amazes me that Casey holds up. Melich should work for the Mossad in Israel. In fact, before I find out he's Portuguese, I think he's Israeli. Melich tried every technique in the book. He is great at what he does. But Casey, the compulsive liar, never cracks."
– Robyn Walensky

"It's still amazing to me how she reacted or how she didn't react inside the interview. There's no question about it. You all have heard the interview. There's times where I can tell myself I was frustrated to the point that she wasn't being honest or completely honest with us. The example of a monster or someone who just committed an accident is a method of interrogation that we learn through various schools, particularly the Reid School and as far as my opinion on it, I won't give my opinion on that, I'm sorry. But suffice to say that she never said it was an accident. That would've been her opportunity to say so had it been. And obviously we give them the ability to explain their actions but they always can come up and say, 'Well, this is what happened.' Even to this day, I'm still surprised that she just didn't come off, that she wouldn't tell us the truth and that's all we were after

was the truth. That day this whole thing could have ended had we known the truth."
– Corporal Yuri Melich at OCSO first and final news conference

"I can tell you I didn't do anything beyond what other law enforcement officers would've done in the country. But I can tell you for a fact, there are hundreds, if not thousands, of law enforcement officers much better and much more capable and better at interviewing in interrogation. I won't even pretend and say I'm top-notch on that. I'd like to think I'm competent on it. I appreciate the accolades I've received for grilling her, but again, I'm just one person out of hundreds of thousands of law enforcement officers who do this work every day."
– Corporal Yuri Melich in interview with Robyn Walensky

"I never seen anything like it. I've been doing this a long time. I've never seen anything like this. Obviously I've talked to a lot of people who have lied to us over the years but I mean, I've talked to a lot of people whose lies were more elaborate and seemed well thought out. I think in this case, it was lying for five more minutes. We watched her lie to get into the back lot. We watched her lie as we walked into the building and ultimately she lied to us. It just seemed like a lie to get five more minutes. Obviously she had to know, as we were walking to the HR building, she didn't have an office there."
– Sergeant John Allen in interview with Robyn Walensky

"Well, let's just say, at twenty-two years old, when I was twenty-two, if I had two grown law enforcement officers in the room with me, I wouldn't have held up as much. I was impressed at the fact that she was maintaining that lie so consistently. The lie about the Zenaida Fernandez-Gonzalez. I couldn't understand why she wouldn't come off it, how she would still cling to that after everything she told us was being shown to be a lie. It was so surreal. I couldn't believe it. So I had to go back and say, you know, she's so adamant about this, maybe there is a Zanny the nanny. So that's why we spent all this time trying to look for Zenaida Gonzalez, Zenaida Fernandez-Gonzalez. We couldn't not pay attention to that. Simply because she was so adamant that that's the person who took her child. So for months until

the indictment we were looking for Zenaida Fernandez-Gonzalez. We had to believe her on that."
– Corporal Yuri Melich in interview with Robyn Walensky

"Well, I don't know that I can rank her. About the interview, I can say this, obviously that morning, Yuri went out in the early morning hours and started the investigation. When he went to Universal to follow up on information that she'd given him, we had a conversation, Detective Wells and I took her out there to Universal, where we talked with her. You guys have the tape. What was said during the interview was said. I think it's important to note that our goal at that point was what was important. I think it's been said by some people, we were desperate. In fact, we were desperate. We were desperate to find a child we were told was missing. And that's what that interview was about. To try to find Caylee Anthony. I would've taken Casey to any theme park she wanted to go to if it would have led to finding her. The interview speaks for itself. We were there to try to get information to try to get Caylee Anthony."
– Sergeant John Allen in OCSO first and final news conference

"Just like the pregnancy, you're faced with reality. You heard what Ms. Drane Burdick said about Casey. She's walking down Universal Studios, 'Ah, come here, this is my office over here, let me walk down this way,' and then faces reality. Well this is the way she was raised. And think about that for a second. She takes law enforcement down this path, down to an office that doesn't exist. This is how this family lives. This is how Casey learned to deal with her problems."
– Jose Baez during his opening statement

"So, in that amazing conversation with Yuri Melich and with John Allen she admits to lying about working at Universal for reasons which are not clear, but maintains the nanny story. 'I'm lying to you about working here but everything else I told you is true.' And she maintains that lie through conversations with law enforcement, she maintains that lie through conversations with her parents and her family, which you saw through all of July and August."
– Prosecutor Jeff Ashton during closing argument

CHAPTER 12

THE SHADY BUNCH

"During the trial I post a picture of the Anthony's in four squares on my Facebook page. George – Cindy – Lee – Casey. And I write, 'This is clearly not the Brady Bunch.' One of my Facebook followers writes, 'You're right, they're more like the Shady Bunch.' The defense, desperate to refute the amazing amount of forensic evidence, is about to throw darts and doubt at the wall and see what sticks. Jose Baez is about to air out all of the Anthony dirty laundry. An alleged affair that George reportedly has with a woman who volunteers to help search for Caylee. The defense strategy is obvious; maybe jurors will think George is a sneak and a liar, and covering up the crime. And while Baez is at it, he's really going to toss father George under the bus with a stunning ear-popping allegation that he sexually molested his own daughter."
– Robyn Walensky

"Casey was raised to lie. This child, at eight years old, learned to lie immediately. She could be thirteen years old, have her father's penis in her mouth and then go to school and play with the other kids."
– Jose Baez

"Normally I write three versions of my radio reports and interchange different pieces of sound in each. Here are the three different leads I write. But the sound is so, so, so compelling. I use it in all three of my radio wraps."
– Robyn Walensky

Lead #1: "Day one brings a bombshell from the defense, a stunning sex 'allegation.' Jose Baez shocking some jurors and everyone else in court with this graphic eye-popping statement about Casey's dad, George." (Penis sound bite is played here NOT bleeped out.)

Lead #2: "Some in court visually disgusted after the shocking opening statement on day one. Jose Baez alleges George Anthony engaged in a sex act with his daughter Casey."
(Penis sound bite is played here NOT bleeped out.)

Lead #3: "An absolute shocking sex allegation, unleashed by the defense. Jose Baez tosses Casey's dad, George, right under the bus."
(Penis sound bite is played here NOT bleeped out.)

"Listeners upset about the 'P word' call WDBO radio to complain… eventually, when the sound bite is used again weeks later…we run the clip of audio with the 'P word' bleeped out. On day one, I also record my radio teases using the same sound…and they go like this: 'A graphic sex allegation takes center stage. (Play penis sound bite.) I'm Robyn Walensky. The shocking details next in just ten minutes.' And to keep it fair, my second tease: 'I'm Robyn Walensky. George Anthony says it's all a lie! (Play sound of George saying he didn't do it.) The story straight ahead in just ten minutes' Radio is all about ratings. The goal is to keep people tuned in.

"So I write crisp for the ear and deliver the sound that will distract drivers to actually pay attention and listen. At the end of the day this is a business, based on how many ears are tuning in. And this is a trial that keeps on giving. At night I am a 'guest' on HLN's Nancy Grace show." **– Robyn Walensky**

"And, also, to Robyn Walensky, WDBO, we now believe there's a very strong possibility tot mom will have to take the stand. Take a listen to this." **– HLN's Nancy Grace, May 25, 2011**

"The penis sound bite is played, the long version."**– Robyn Walensky**

"Casey was raised to lie. This child at eight years old learned to lie immediately. She could be thirteen years old, have her father's penis in her mouth and then go to school and play with the other kids as if nothing ever happened. Nothing's wrong. That will help you understand why no one knew that her child was dead. That's the most important thing you must keep in the back of your mind, is that sex abuse does things to us. It changes you. As soon as Casey came around this corner and went back, she saw George Anthony holding Caylee in his arms. She immediately grabbed Caylee and began to cry and cry and cry. And shortly thereafter, George began to yell at her. (Baez raises his voice very loud.) 'Look what you've done! Your mother will never forgive you, and you will go to jail for child neglect for the rest of your frikkin' life!'" **– Jose Baez**

"Robyn Walensky, let me get this straight. The theory is she was in denial because she was molested as a child and, therefore, she left her two-year-old alone with George Anthony and, therefore, all these string of witnesses we saw in court today are to testify to her denial? She never even mentioned Caylee's existence."**– HLN's Nancy Grace**

"Nancy, in a million years, any woman—you know this—who is sexually abused or even is suspicious of an older man in some kind of way, if a guy looks at you the wrong way, in a million years, are you going to leave your child with that person if that's true? That is just against the laws of human nature." **– Robyn Walensky**

"Have you ever sexually molested your daughter, Casey Anthony?" **– Prosecutor Jeff Ashton to witness George Anthony**

"No, sir." **– George Anthony**

"Things are at such a low point, Anthony family attorney Mark Lippman releases the following statement." **– Robyn Walensky**

"George and Cindy Anthony are shocked and appalled that the defense would resort to lies about them in today's opening statement.

Baez's idle speculation today certainly are not facts. The only result achieved by the defense in this statement was to further hurt this grieving family. George Anthony maintains that he never had anything to do with the death of Caylee Marie Anthony, including what happened to her remains after she allegedly drowned. The sworn testimony given today shows that he has never wavered about his knowledge regarding these events. He, like the rest of the Anthony family, only seeks the truth about what happened to their granddaughter."

– Mark Lippman, lawyer for George and Cindy Anthony

"With respect to the sexual abuse allegations, the only thing that we have to indicate that there was any sexual abuse would be Casey's word."

– Sergeant John Allen

"If he (Jose Baez) made those allegations, there's nothing in my investigation that supports anything along those lines."

– Corporal Yuri Melich

"But in the end, Casey's words toward her dad debunk all of this utter nonsense."   **– Robyn Walensky**

"I can't say this enough to you. You're the best father and by far the best grandfather I ever met. I mean that with all my heart."

– Casey Anthony in jailhouse interview with her parents

"And the twisting of the truth is about to continue in court. Rumor has it, the Defense is going to go down a possible 'Caylee died by accident' road. Here's how I teased the story for the WDBO audience in my first radio report 'tease.'"   **– Robyn Walensky**

"Eleventh-hour bombshell. The defense might claim Caylee killed by accident! I'm Robyn Walensky outside the courthouse. All the breaking details as DAY ONE of the trial starts straight ahead in just ten minutes. And then TEASE 2: "Eleventh-hour stunner. The defense files discovery on the eve of trial and may claim CAYLEE was killed by accident! I'm Robyn Walensky outside the courthouse. All the breaking details straight ahead in just ten minutes."

– Robyn Walensky, reports on air

"And then the bombshell we've all been waiting for. Jose Baez, during his opening argument, about to tell the jury, and the world, 'how' he believes Caylee really died."

– Robyn Walensky

"How in the world can a mother wait thirty days before ever reporting her child missing? That's insane, that's bizarre. The answer is actually relatively simple. She never was missing. Caylee Anthony died on June 16, 2008, when she drowned in her family's swimming pool."

– Jose Baez

"It's not really surprising considering the fact that they had to come up with something new. We conducted a very thorough investigation and it was not said to us Caylee met an untimely end early on and for them to come up with this new story at the eleventh hour of the drowning, I can't say it shocked us but you know, it is what it is."

– Corporal Yuri Melich

"Swimming pool? What? Miraculously, Baez can kind of support his 'pool theory.' Cindy will say she told Corporal Yuri Melich that she remembers coming home from work to let the dogs outside and notices the ladder on the pool (instead of on the ground) and remembers the side gate is open. She recalls telling co-workers about it the next day. Cindy will testify she remembers Caylee went swimming on June 15, it was chilly, and then she's 100 percent sure she put the ladder down."

– Robyn Walensky

"Within twenty-four hours, Cindy Anthony tells Detective Melich, who is the lead detective in this case, about the ladder incident. And it goes ignored. There's no follow-up. No questions asked. No information gathered. No forensics. Nothing. It's ignored. They're more concerned with the transport, the alleged transport of the car, than they are with what actually happened."

– Jose Baez during his opening statement

"But as sportscaster Warner Wolf would say when you 'go to the video tape,' Jose Baez's pool drowning theory is dismissed by none other than Casey herself." **– Robyn Walensky**

"Dad's blowing up at the media. Someone said that the baby just drowned in the pool."
– Cindy Anthony in a jailhouse video conversation with Casey

"Oh, surprise, surprise."
– Casey Anthony to mom Cindy in jailhouse video conversation

"But it's this shady odd family dynamic that Baez continues to beat the drum on." **– Robyn Walensky**

"What makes this case unique is the family that it happened to. You will hear stories about a family that is incredibly dysfunctional, you will hear about ugly things, secret things, things that people don't speak about." **– Jose Baez**

"On June 16, 2008, after Caylee died, Casey did what she's been doing all her life—hiding her pain, going into that dark corner, and pretending that she does not live in the situation that she's living in… It all began when Casey was eight years old and her father came into her room and began to touch her inappropriately and it escalated."
– Jose Baez

"George Anthony, the first witness called in the trial, denies the defense team's allegations that he ever abused his daughter, Casey Anthony. He says that today's opening statements are the first time he ever heard about Caylee's alleged drowning."
– Robyn Walensky

"When I heard that today, it hurt really bad. If I would have known something happened to Caylee, I wouldn't be here today. I would have done everything humanly possible to save my granddaughter if what was stated prior really happened." **– George Anthony**

"Casey Anthony was raised to lie," Baez says. He adds, "Sex abuse does things to us, it changes you. She's not guilty of murder. This is not a murder case. This is a sad, tragic accident that snowballed out of control."
– Jose Baez

"Jose Baez goes on with his 'story.' He claims after pulling Caylee from the pool, George Anthony screams and goes off on Casey."
– Robyn Walensky

"Look what you've done. Your mother will never forgive you. You'll go to jail for the rest of your life."
– Jose Baez

"It's dramatic. But not believable. The entire tale seems made up after the fact."
– Robyn Walensky

"You'll see evidence, conclusive evidence, that he took steps to throw his own daughter under the bus just to protect himself." **– Jose Baez**

"Baez goes on in his opening statement about the gas cans. His theory is George Anthony reported them missing from his shed to point the investigation toward Casey. On the gas cans, the same duct tape is found wrapped around Caylee's head. Prosecutors say Casey stole the gas cans from the shed. But gas cans aren't really the issue, it's George's alleged affair that takes center stage. Baez claims George suggests to his alleged mistress that Caylee's death is an accident."
– Robyn Walensky

"George began to break down and cry and she asked him what happened to Caylee and he said it was an accident that snowballed out of control. This is before Caylee was ever found."
– Jose Baez

"George Anthony, retired cop, comes off as a grieving grandfather. But what man in front of his wife, kids, and the entire world admits he's had an affair? Especially with a woman whose street name is 'River Cruz.'"
–Robyn Walensky

"George told me, I believe it was an accident that spun out of control. Or snowballed, snowballed out of control."

– Krystal Holloway aka River Cruz

"George Anthony, a retired, clean-cut cop, in shape, silver hair, tan skin, neatly dressed, comes off looking like a really bad guy and a really big liar. From my view, the prosecutors totally underestimate the credibility of Krystal Holloway aka River Cruz. She doesn't have the look, but doesn't appear to be lying. She testifies she has an affair with George Anthony. And I believe every word. More importantly, it seems the jurors buy her story too. This is bad for prosecutors. The defense team paints father George as a dishonest man and scores bigtime. But in my opinion, just because he won't admit he cheated on his wife in front of his family and the world, doesn't make him a baby killer."

– Robyn Walensky

"I need you in my life"

– George Anthony in a text message to Krystal Holloway the night of Caylee's memorial service

"I never had a romantic affair with Krystal Holloway or River Cruz or any name she wanted to give you or the world."

– George Anthony, denying he had an intimate relationship with Krystal Holloway

"But in pouring through countless documents provided by the state attorney's office for research on this project, I learn from an OCSO supplemental report that when Krystal Holloway shows up at the 'Kid Finders' tent, she identifies herself to George as 'River,' a nickname she's used for twelve years. The two exchange numbers, spend time at the tent and later at her residence while she is there alone. A security guard at the apartment complex is interviewed by OCSO detectives and states George Anthony definitely came to visit—in the time frame between late 2008 and early 2009—and then at some point in 2009, the guard is instructed by Holloway to no longer allow George into the subdivision."

– Robyn Walensky

"Did you develop a relationship with Mr. Anthony?"

– Jose Baez

"Yes, sir. I did."   **– Krystal Holloway**

"Was this an intimate relationship?"   **– Jose Baez**

"Yes."   **– Krystal Holloway**

"She is extremely credible on the stand."   **– Robyn Walensky**

"He was sitting on my couch and I was sitting on the floor and he had said it was an accident that snowballed out of control. But, I was in shock, and by the time I looked up, his eyes were filled with tears and I didn't elaborate, I didn't ask him anything further."
– Krystal Holloway

"Was this before Caylee was found?"   **– Jose Baez**

"Yes, sir, it was around Thanksgiving time, I believe."
– Krystal Holloway

"When the Anthony's held their memorial for Caylee Anthony, were you still in a relationship with George Anthony?"   **– Jose Baez**

"Yes."   **– Krystal Holloway**

"Can you read the date of that text message to the ladies and gentlemen of the jury and then its contents."   **– Jose Baez**

"Tuesday Dec 16…from George Anthony…just thinking about you…I need you in my life."   **– Krystal Holloway**

"Father George is critical to the case. He is the last person to see Caylee alive on June 16 in the afternoon before he leaves for work. Caylee is walking out the door with Casey. The next time anyone sees Casey is later that same night on surveillance video at Blockbuster, renting a movie with her boyfriend Jesse Grund. No sign of Caylee on the surveillance video. Caylee will never be seen alive again."
– Robyn Walensky

"The defense has a bull's-eye on George Anthony and it's clear as soon as Jose Baez begins his opening argument, father George is about to get thrown under the bus and buried there." **– Robyn Walensky**

"George told me I believe it was an accident that spun out of control. Or snowballed, snowballed out of control." **– Krystal Holloway**

"I'm not convinced what George said or didn't say. But I know one thing, these two were definitely involved. I watch River Cruz's body language and it's clear she is telling the truth about having an intimate relationship with George. And there is language in a text message to support her story." **– Robyn Walensky**

"The night of Caylee's memorial service he texts me, 'I need you in my life.'" **– Krystal Holloway**

Cindy & George Anthony arrive at the Orange County Courthouse
Photo Courtesy: Robyn Walensky

News Crews follow Cindy & George Anthony at the
Orange County Courthouse
Photo Courtesy: Robyn Walensky

"Although it appears her marriage to George has had its ups and downs, the couple is always seen at the courthouse holding hands. Despite everything George has put Cindy through, allegations of affairs, gambling away their money, a suicide attempt, Cindy still appears to be loyal to him, at least on the surface while the cameras are rolling. The one thing though that is obvious from photos, her tearful testimony, and her body language on the stand, is that Cindy Anthony never wavers in her devotion to her granddaughter, Caylee. In her early testimony at trial she falls apart when her 9-1-1 call is played, her head literally in her hand, and from the courtroom spectator seats you can only see the top of her blonde hair. She looks so loving in all of the pool pictures with Caylee. A younger-looking Cindy in her bathing suit, walking up the ladder with little Caylee, and always right by her side in the family pool. It reminds me of my own grandmother Sally, never more than a step away from me when I was that age. It's Cindy who buys all of Caylee's cute clothes, feeds her, buys her toys, and decorates her room with the Winnie the Pooh theme. That said, the computer searches for chloroform done inside the Anthony home are problematic. In a supplemental report done by the Orange County Sheriff's Office, one of Casey's ex's, Ricardo Morales, tells investigators Casey once joked about giving Caylee 'baby medicine' to put her to sleep. Investigators find a photo with the caption, "win her over with chloroform" on Morales' MySpace page. He says he never did it, but found it funny so he posted it. Much has been made about the number of chloroform searches on the Anthony home computer. Was it searched eighty-four times? Was it searched once? or twice? To me the number is irrelevant; someone was looking up how to make chloroform. Perhaps they jotted down or memorized the directions on how to put together the brew. But with Casey facing death, Cindy turns and takes the hit for Casey, lying on the stand about her whereabouts when these searches for chloroform and neck breaking are done from the family computer. The searches taking place almost four months before Caylee goes missing. This is why prosecutors call it premeditated murder."

– Robyn Walensky

"Do you recall in March of 2008 you doing any types of searches for any items that might include chloroform?" **– Jose Baez**

"Yes, and I started looking up chloroform, I mean chlorophyll, and then that prompted me to look up chloroform."

– Cindy Anthony on the witness stand at trial

"Chloroform is a chemical compound that can be used to knock someone unconscious and also is found in human decomposition. Cindy comes up with this preposterous scenario, claiming she looked up chloroform while searching for info on chlorophyll, a green pigment found in plants. Cindy testifies her dogs may have been eating bamboo leaves containing chlorophyll. And I'm the pope. But

Cindy is a nurse and her bosses testify at trial. They say records clearly show she is logged in at her job and the computer evidence shows she was at her desk at work when the Internet search or searches take place miles away inside her home. So who is lying ?

I feel bad for her on some level. I see Cindy Anthony every day in court as she sits next to husband George in the fourth row. As the trial nears an end I run into her in the twenty-third-floor ladies room, before court gets under way at 8:30 a.m. I never acknowledge her, but on more than one occasion, I can see, she is crying. Testimony for the day has not even started yet. I cannot imagine the pain she is in. One day in court as she gets off the stand, she turns toward the defense table and mouths "I love you" as she walks past Casey. These three words despite the fact her granddaughter is dead and the state says her daughter did it. On another day, I ride up in a very crowded elevator. George is in the corner by the elevator buttons, and Cindy is standing cradled around him with both arms. This is the closest I've stood next to her and I see she's wearing a butterfly necklace and a bracelet to remember Caylee. George and Cindy look like a couple, and are trying to act like a couple, but the vibe you get is they are together and faking it because of the trial. And then there's Casey's brother, Lee."
– Robyn Walensky

"I was just angry at everyone in general that they didn't, that they didn't want to include me."
– Lee Anthony, Casey's brother, cries on the stand as he's questioned about not being at Caylee's birth

"Brother Lee Anthony comes off as an emotional basket case. On the day he breaks down in court, the tears running down his face don't match the words coming out of his mouth. He is crying about being lied to about his sister's pregnancy, being left out of his sister's shower, and not being present at Caylee's birth. I don't know one guy this age or any age that would cry like this. Most men would be happy to be left alone. The emotion just doesn't add up. From my view, brother Lee comes off like he's hiding something and crying about something else. But I do not believe for a minute he sexually abused his sister as the defense alleges."
– Robyn Walensky

CHAPTER 13

HER KNIGHT IN SHINNG ARMOR

"Really?"
– Lead defense attorney Jose Baez speaks to Casey Anthony during jury selection in Clearwater, Florida, May 9, 2011

"Really."
– Casey Anthony answers Jose Baez

"You're acting like a two-year-old."
– Jose Baez scolds his client Casey

"He is visibly aggravated. As he turns the page on his yellow legal pad, the paper makes noise. Seconds later, Casey taps his left elbow with the back of her right hand and quickly pulls away. Jose makes a face, looks disgusted, agitated, and uncomfortable sitting next to his client at the defense table. What they're talking about we'll never know. But there is clearly tension between these two, and Casey ends up changing seats. The next day she sits as far away from Jose as she can."
– Robyn Walensky

Jose Baez arrives at the Orange County Courthouse
Photo Courtesy: Robyn Walensky

"The first time I get to ask Jose Baez a question is at a Hispanic Journalist Breakfast here in Orlando a few weeks before the trial starts. A woman in a black sports car with tinted windows drops him off—then later picks him up. He sits and sips espresso and seems super comfortable taking questions in Spanish then in English from reporters at this on-the-record event. This is the first time I hear Baez's name mentioned in the same sentence as Geraldo. A Spanish-speaking reporter asks Baez about his relationship with Rivera and it dawns on me Baez must be getting some free tips from his friend, the veteran broadcaster, on his outfits and managing the media. To my eye, Baez is definitely looking spiffier. Expensive suits, and better coordinated shirts, ties, and hankies. But during jury selection in Clearwater, it is not Baez's appearance that catches my attention anymore; it's his odd interaction with client Casey. In videotaped calls from jail with her parents, Casey adoringly and with familiarity calls

her lawyer 'Jose.' As the days wear on in Clearwater, Casey appears visibly agitated at the defense table, pointing and yelling at him. And I think, 'What woman, not involved with a man on an intimate level, yells at a man like that and gets in his face?" I answer my own question: 'Only a woman involved in a relationship; real, or imagined, would lash out that way.' The next day I come to court and the defense team plays musical chairs. Casey sits as far away from 'Jose' as possible. They are separated by the rest of her 'dream team.' My brain flashes back to videos from 2008, when Casey is briefly out on bond. She wears tight shorts and sunglasses, brings baked goods to Baez's law office, and spends endless hours there. While many privately and publicly speculate about this lawyer/client relationship. This is one of the shortest chapters in Beautiful Life? as the truth is, only they know."
– Robyn Walensky

CHAPTER 14

TWO TEAMS

"It reminds me of color-war at camp. Two teams. Different outfits. Different goals. Different strategies. Distinctly different in demeanor. Singing different songs. And dancing to a totally different tune. Both hoping to win the competition. A complete contrast. The prosecutors appearing prepared and completely in sync at every turn. The defense appearing scattered and not on the same page. Lawyers representing the State of Florida; The lead prosecutor in the case assistant state attorney Linda Drane Burdick. Assistant state attorneys Jeff Ashton and Frank George complete the prosecution team. This trio appears unified, organized and ready to win. Burdick delivers a succinct and memorable opening statement. She details the thirty-one days Casey doesn't report Caylee missing and repeats, "Where is Caylee?" at the close of every paragraph. With great emphasis on the words: "Where—is—Caylee?" Jeff Ashton handles the science, the forensic aspects of this case. He becomes known for wearing a different colorful theme tie every day to court. He's always smart and always a bit snarky. During Jose Baez's closing statement, Ashton will smirk and laugh and get called out on his antics by Baez who calls him "the laughing man." Judge Perry has these two grown men who are acting like school kids watch the video tape. There are apologies all around and the trial moves continue. On a prior occasion, when Perry asks both men to look at the clock and tell him what time it is, they give different answers. Baez tells the judge, 'See, we can't agree on anything.' So true. Frank George reminds me of some of my personal attorney friends who aren't flashy, but equally love the law, and have all their T's crossed and I's dotted. George is professional, methodical, and detail oriented as he cross-examines witnesses. George is well dressed and polite but extremely low-key compared to Jeff Ashton. But a solid team consists of various personalities and strengths that operate in unison.

Casey Anthony's defense dream team is a mixed bag of talent and level of experience. Lead counsel for the defense is Jose Baez. Read his resume and you will notice the Florida criminal defense attorney has limited experience. Veteran defense attorney Cheney Mason, the oldest member on the team, brought in because of his vast experience and the fact he is death penalty qualified. There's attorney Dorothy Clay Sims who basically winds up being Casey Anthony's babysitter in court. One day I listen to Sims in court. I'm sitting in the first row right behind her and can barely hear what she is saying. Sims has a very soft voice and can barely hold anyone's attention, but she holds Casey's hand, literally throughout the proceedings, beginning at jury selection until the big 'not guilty' embrace at the end of the trial. She becomes a 'mother figure' to Casey. And she provides a shoulder for Casey to literally lean and cry on. Finally, there's Ann Finnell, the death penalty expert. She's around every day during jury selection in Clearwater but is only seen at the trial in Orlando a few times. In Pinellas County she's the defense attorney who questions potential jurors about their views on the death penalty. Are they for it? Against it? For it under certain circumstances? Totally against it no matter what? The friendly grilling all as Casey Anthony sits at the defense table alert and awaiting her fate." **– Robyn Walensky**

CHAPTER 15

COSMETICS COUNT

Casey Anthony partying during 31 days Caylee is missing
"Florida State Attorney's Office, 9th Judicial Circuit"

"Petite and pale. The first time I see Casey in court, I'm struck by her appearance. She's so slight and so washed out. I think how shabby she looks compared to the party pics seen round the world. The sexy shots of her scantily clad dancing on stage with men and women in low-cut tops during the hot body shot contest at club Fusion. But in person, here in court, she has an evil aura. Her face is blank, but you get the sense she's thinking. I wonder, does she replay what really happened on June 16ᵗ 2008, over and over again? During jury selection, she compulsively plays with pieces of her hair, which are falling in her face, drooping from both sides of her head. Her hands repeatedly trying to push the hair back. Over and over again. Almost like a nervous tick. It's so distracting to watch. So much so, that I'm clearly not the only person who notices this and these pieces of hair are eventually pulled back neater at trial. On the few occasions we hear it, Casey's voice is soft and doesn't match her sharp exterior. Her dark hair contrasts greatly with her white skin. There is something clearly not right with this woman who I stare at for long periods of time. Most disturbing to my critical eye, she's able to go from giggly and silly to somber and stern in less than a millisecond. Honestly, it's scary to watch. I am completely convinced she could be loving one second then totally snap. After watching her in court it also doesn't surprise me that she's able to conduct herself around her friends as if nothing catastrophic has happened."

– Robyn Walensky

Casey Anthony partying during 31 days Caylee is missing
"Florida State Attorney's Office, 9th Judicial Circuit"

"Trial day two, and jurors see Casey Anthony, again, looking drab and washed up, wearing a white blouse with a ruffle. On the stand are roommates of her then boyfriend Tony Lazzaro's. These guys are witnesses for the state. All testify to Casey's demeanor during the days in June of '08 Caylee was missing. All say Casey cooked and cleaned in their apartment. Never seemed distraught, depressed, or angry. And, was out partying at Orlando nightclubs."
**– Robyn Walensky, WDBO Radio report,
day two of Casey Anthony trial**

"What also strikes me is her incredibly narcissistic behavior on the jailhouse videos. Nancy Grace gets into this on her show on June third."
– Robyn Walensky

"We hear tot mom describing how she's the victim, not Caylee. We are taking your calls live. Out to Robyn, Walensky, reporter, WDBO. Robyn, what a day in the courtroom. How is the jury responding as all of this just poured into evidence?"
– HLN's Nancy Grace

"Nancy, I was sitting in the front row when these three videos were played. And I have to tell you, in video number three, the one you're referencing, where she gets all frustrated with the parents—Nancy, it's all about her. She's the victim. And one of the jurors—at least one, possibly two—I remember them looking up from their monitors, and then looking at Casey Anthony for a reaction, and she's sitting there like stone."
– Robyn Walensky on CNN's Nancy Grace, June 3

"Describe tot mom's reaction for the viewers, Robyn."
– HLN's Nancy Grace

"She basically has no reaction during this. The only time she ever really cries in court, Nancy, is when it's all about her, when she sees herself crying. But today, when this is going on, when she's acting like the victim in this third video, which is a month into her lockup—she's been locked up at this point for a month—you can see her on the tape visibly getting angry, frustrated with the parents.

Yet she's sitting in court like she's another person, like it`s her twin sister."   **– Robyn Walensky on HLN's Nancy Grace, June 3**

"What we are showing you right now is tot mom as she heard this jailhouse tape played. You`re hearing it just as the jury did. Take a listen."   **– HLN's Nancy Grace**

"I need to be looked at as a victim because I`m just as much of a victim—OK... I`m just as much of a victim as the rest of you. And it hasn`t been portrayed that way and it probably won`t be. But I know that and at least there are other people that know that and understand that."   **– Casey Anthony, jailhouse video**

"I was in Lake County two days ago."   **– Cindy Anthony**

"OK."   **– Casey Anthony**

"Is there anything there?"   **– Cindy Anthony**

"Mom! Jesus! I`m sorry. I love you guys. I miss you."   **– Casey Anthony**

"All right, sweetheart. Here`s Dad."   **– Cindy Anthony**

"No, I`m going hang up. I want to just walk away right now because..."   **– Casey Anthony**

"Please don't."   **– Cindy Anthony**

"I`m frustrated and I`m angry. And I don`t want to be angry. This is the first time I`ve truly, truly been angry this entire time. But I`m so beyond frustrated with all of this that I can`t even swallow right now, it hurts."   **– Casey Anthony**

CHAPTER 16

THE SNAKE AND THE SKULL

"Dispatch, we found a human skull."

"Oh my gosh."

"Uh, skull of a... that we believe to be human."

"What's the location?"

"It's right off Suburban and Chickasaw. In the Caylee Anthony area, right by the school."

"Ohhh..."

"Roy Kronk is the local meter reader that calls cops three times, August 11, 12, and 13 of 2008, to report he sees something suspicious in the woods near the Anthony home. Kronk says he goes to take a leak in the woods and stumbles on the skull. Kronk says, 'We didn't really have bathroom facilities,' and that's when he says he spotted 'an object that appeared a little odd to me.' Kronk calls his co-workers to check it out but they spot a rattlesnake and become preoccupied with the serpent. (Kronk will eventually sell a licensed picture of the dead snake for a 'reported' $15,000 dollars and do a national TV interview.) Kronk calls the police again and is told to call the Caylee Anthony tip line, which he does, but does not receive a

call back. Then when Kronk calls the third time, a deputy responds to the scene. His name is Richard Cain, at the time he's forty years old, and has been employed by OCSO since June 2, 2006. It's 15:37:52. Three thirty-seven in the afternoon. Kronk shows the deputy where to look."
– Robyn Walensky

"He went to the water's edge. I pointed to where it was at. He just swept his head back and forth and said, 'I don't see anything.' And pretty much, that was it. I guess the deputy didn't want to go in the water to look at the bag."
– Meter reader Roy Kronk in a television interview on ABC's Good Morning America

"Kronk says Deputy Cain pulled out his expandable metal baton, walked to the water's edge and dismissed the bag as 'trash.' So in a nutshell, Roy Kronk is basically blown off by Deputy Cain."
– Robyn Walensky

"The cop was, I would say, he was kind of rude to me. And I am just trying to help out, and I'm trying to be a nice guy and instead I am catching all this so I just didn't care anymore."
– Meter reader Roy Kronk in a television interview on ABC's Good Morning America

"Records show at 16:02:21 …4:02 p.m., twenty minutes later, Cain wraps up at the woods scene. Deputy Cain is reassigned to a desk job after failing to properly follow up on Kronk's tip. Turns out Deputy Cain had two complaints filed against him, one in 2006 and another in 2007, both for failing to 'properly investigate an incident.' An internal police investigation finds Cain failed to thoroughly investigate the woods scene in August of 2008, therefore possibly delaying the Caylee Anthony investigation for months. The review recommends the OCSO terminate Cain. In May 2009, Cain 'resigns.' Forward up the clock four months to December 11, 2008. Kronk calls police again to report he sees what he thinks is a skull. Eight days later DNA tests indicate it is Caylee."
– Robyn Walensky

"They've been really hard on me. You try to do the right thing, you try to be the nice guy and you just get vilified. I mean, the sad thing is people believe some of the things that are being said. And I have nothing to do with this at all. I tried to help put a little closure to that poor child. And she got a decent burial at the end of all this. That's what I tried to do."
– Meter reader Roy Kronk in a television interview on ABC's Good Morning America

"The defense will tell jurors Roy Kronk tampered with Caylee's remains."
– Robyn Walensky

"Mr. Kronk is a morally bankrupt individual who actually took Caylee's body and hid her."
– Jose Baez

"Baez goes on to tell the jurors, Kronk hoped to collect reward money. There is also an allegation Roy Kronk had insider information as to where to look for the body. There was a rumor going around that his girlfriend, who works in the Orange County Jail, overhead a conversation about where Caylee's body was."
– Robyn Walensky

"Well, I think that's purely speculation on someone's part. The only person that probably definitely could tell you where that body was the person who put it there. And I am not aware of any information that indicated that Roy Kronk heard it from some other third party or second party in this case."
– Sheriff Jerry Demings during post-trial news conference

"Logic will tell you, had the officer who responded to the original call back in August taken Kronk's claim seriously, Caylee might have been found sooner and there may have been soft tissue left to do tests on to see if chloroform was in her body. And, perhaps, like in almost every episode of CSI, there would have been fresh fingerprints still lingering on the duct tape, leading to the hands of Caylee's killer."
– Robyn Walensky

"We learned on December 17 that Roy Kronk had called back in August. To sit here and speculate what we could've found, what we couldn't have found. I don't know what we could have found. I'd like to say we could have found more but no one would know unless we could go back and change time, what we would have actually found at that time. The body was there in August of 2008. It would've been two months as opposed to six months. So I'd like to think we could find more. But again, to say for certain, who knows?"
– Corporal Yuri Melich during an OCSO news conference

CHAPTER 17

BELLA VITA = "BEAUTIFUL LIFE"

"I did her first tattoo when she was eighteen." **- Tattoo artist Bobby Williams, manager of Cast Iron Tattoos**

Close-up of Casey Anthony's "Bella Vita" Tattoo
"Florida State Attorney's Office, 9th Judicial Circuit"

"Her child is missing, yet Casey Anthony is out and about, getting a Tattoo. It's July 2, 2008, and she pays $60 cash to Bobby Williams to ink 'Bella Vita,' Italian for 'Beautiful Life,' on her left shoulder. When he finishes, Casey pays for a pizza and the two chow down."

– Robyn Walensky

"She didn't seem upset or anything. She was happy for the most part."

– Bobby Williams, manager of Cast Iron Tattoos, tells jurors on the stand

"I don't recall specifically how we heard it. I remember Yuri coming to me and telling me that we had uncovered a witness, how we had spoken to somebody who got the statement that she had gone to a tattoo parlor during this time. One of the things that we did during this period was, Eric Edwards was tasked with the responsibility of doing a time line, collecting statements, and trying to put Casey in different places during the time when the child was missing. And that time line, that effort to put that time line together, really uncovered a lot of this."

– Sergeant John Allen

"I already knew what it meant. I've been doing tattoos for eleven years so it's not the first time I've actually done that tattoo, 'Bella Vita.' I've done it maybe about a half a dozen times."

– Bobby Williams, manager of Cast Iron Tattoos

"Yuri and I went back to the jail with a search warrant to photograph it. We had a court order to photograph it."

– Sergeant John Allen

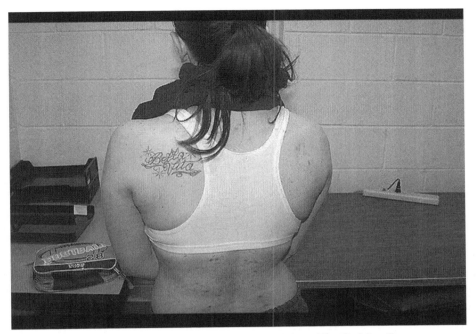

Casey Anthony told to reveal her "Bella Vita"
Tattoo so it can be photographed in Jail
"Florida State Attorney's Office, 9th Judicial Circuit"

"She didn't disrobe totally. She had a tank top on and CSI Jennifer Welch actually went in and took the photographs and I was actually there as a witness to see it just so I can explain in detail what it was."
– Corporal Yuri Melich

"I would say it's more or less to memorialize life, just like, living life or how beautiful life is."
– Bobby Williams, manager of Cast Iron Tattoos

"OK, you see it and you think?"
– Robyn Walensky in interview with Corporal Yuri Melich

"Surreal. Why would somebody get a tattoo of a 'beautiful life' three weeks after their child – in their words – died as a result of an accident in a pool. I couldn't understand why she would even think to do that. Why would you go out and get a tattoo of 'beautiful life' when your child is missing? And I guess, in the defense's own words, 'The child drowned,' and you're going to go out and a get a tattoo of 'a beautiful life.' It doesn't make sense." **– Corporal Yuri Melich**

"And what does 'Bella Vita' mean to you?"
– Robyn Walensky in interview with Sergeant John Allen

"A wonderful life, a beautiful life." **– Sergeant John Allen**

"What do you think it meant to her?" **– Robyn Walensky**

"A wonderful life, a beautiful life." **– Sergeant John Allen**

"Now that I killed my kid? I mean, you tell me." **– Robyn Walensky**

"I'm a father so I can only speak for myself in this regard, if one of my children were missing or one of my children were dead, I don't know that the first thing I'd want to do would be to go get a tattoo. But that's just me personally. If one of my children were missing or dead, I'd be devastated." **– Sergeant John Allen**

"It's 12:45 a.m. and from the time I arrive on scene, my first idea is that even talking to her, maybe she was tired of dealing with the child, she gave it to someone, she just didn't want her parents to see the child. It's just the simple fact that she was happy now that she was able to live the 'beautiful life.'" **– Corporal Yuri Melich**

"Casey returns to the tat parlor on July 15 to schedule another appointment for a few days later." **– Robyn Walensky**

"The fact is that when Casey came in, she was just like everyone else; just normal, happy, she didn't seem distressed about anything when she sat down to get the tattoo."
– Bobby Williams, manager of Cast Iron Tattoos

CHAPTER 18

JUDGE PERRY AND POP-TARTS

"In complete command from day one of all of the courtroom action, antics, and outbursts is Chief Judge Belvin Perry. From my perspective he is fair and funny. He's serious, but sweet. He'd crack everyone up with his 'Perry-isms.' 'Don't go there, Mr. Baez' (with emphasis on the Z). 'I don't want the jury to have to pop in and out like Pop-Tarts.' Then there's the famous Perry-ism: "O-kay" (with an upward high pitch on kay). This is always the signal it's time for lunch or a quick recess. There's emphasis and excitement in his tone. Other Perry-isms: "You MAY,' 'What exhibits ya'll talking about, I can't navigate in darkness,' and 'Ya'll will have seven minutes each to flap ya'll gums.' Then there's Perry's adoring pronunciation of words including the name of the defendant "Miss Anfony." Ya gotta to love this guy. He's totally endearing. But as far as the business of the court, I have never witnessed a judge who can off-the-cuff cite chapter and verse on the law. This man knows his stuff and is in complete command on the bench. He also does not suffer fools well."

– Robyn Walensky

"Sir, are you juror #3207?… Sir, did you hear my instructions this morning when I indicated to you, you are not to discuss this matter with anyone?… What did you do during lunch hour? "
– Judge Belvin Perry, Jr.

"I guess I talked to somebody."
– Juror Jonathan Green

"In Pinellas County during jury selection Perry finds juror Jonathan Green (who works at a Publix Supermarket) in contempt of court after he speaks with a reporter outside the Justice Center, hoping to get out of jury duty. Perry fines him $450."
– Robyn Walensky

"She killed somebody anyway."
– Elizabeth Ann Rogers, out-of-control spectator in Pinellas County courtroom

"The second incident in Pinellas; an outrageous outburst. A heavy-set woman without her shoes on suddenly starts shouting. Deputies respond immediately and escort her out. The woman claims to be on prescription Thorazine and Methadone. After a brief recess she stands before Judge Perry."
– Robyn Walensky

"I've never been in a courtroom like this. I have a three-year-old son. I'm very sorry. I never meant anything like this. I apologize. I will never do this again. I am bipolar, manic depressive, post-traumatic stress."
– Elizabeth Ann Rogers, out-of-control spectator in Pinellas County courtroom

"Judge Perry sentences her to two days in jail for contempt of court."
– Robyn Walensky

"Normally I'd sentence you to 179 days in Pinellas County Jail."
– Judge Belvin Perry, Jr.

"And the courtroom antics aren't over. They say all things come in threes and there is a third incident. In Orange County, a guy who sits quietly in the seat directly behind me during the morning court session decides to act up during the afternoon. The TGI Friday's waiter, flips prosecutor Jeff Ashton the bird. And Judge Perry loses his patience, sentencing this flip-the-finger fool to six days in jail."

– Robyn Walensky

"OK, sir, will you state your name and age." **– Judge Belvin Perry, Jr.**

"My name is Matthew Bartlett, and I'm twenty-eight years old."

– Matthew Bartlett, disruptive observer

"What is that symbol that you are projecting with your fingers?"

– Judge Belvin Perry, Jr.

"I'm using my middle finger." **– Matthew Bartlett, disruptive observer**

"And what does that mean, sir—when you extend one's middle finger?" **– Judge Belvin Perry, Jr.**

"The f-word to some." **– Matthew Bartlett, disruptive observer**

"What does it mean to you, sir, not to some, but to you?"

– Judge Belvin Perry, Jr.

"To use the f-word." **– Matthew Bartlett, disruptive observer**

"And who were you extending the finger to?"

– Judge Belvin Perry, Jr.

"Mr. Ashton." **– Matthew Bartlett, disruptive observer**

"And what was Mr. Ashton doing at that time sir?"

– Judge Belvin Perry, Jr.

"Um." **– Matthew Bartlett, disruptive observer**

"Court was in session, was it not?"   **– Judge Belvin Perry, Jr.**

"Yes, it was."   **– Matthew Bartlett, disruptive observer**

At this point Judge Perry holds up the white sign with bright red writing on it that is posted outside on the door of Courtroom 23, indicating there are to be no gestures or facial expressions inside of any kind while court is in session. Perry is not done with this finger flipping fool. The best is yet to come."   **– Robyn Walensky**

"How far have you gone in school?   **– Judge Belvin Perry, Jr.**

"Twelfth grade."   **– Matthew Bartlett, disruptive observer**

"Can you read and write? Did you not read this sign?"
                                    – Judge Belvin Perry, Jr.

"Judge Perry finds Bartlett guilty of direct criminal contempt. As sheriff's deputies handcuff Bartlett, Perry sentences him to six days in jail and orders him to pay a $400 dollar fine plus court costs. I just shake my head at the sheer stupidity of it all. Have people not been following how strict Judge Perry is ? He's a law-and-order guy. Follow the law or pay the price. Period."   **– Robyn Walensky**

"I'm truly sorry for doing this. This is something stupid. I'm not sure why I even did it."   **– Matthew Bartlett**

"I say on WDBO the next morning in my live shot... 'What an idiot.'"
                                    – Robyn Walensky

CHAPTER 19

PICKING IN PINELLAS

"It's May 9, 2011. For two weeks jurors will be weeded out. It's a painfully slow process and the clock is ticking. Judge Perry reserves this courtroom for two weeks and he's almost out of jurors. Why? Because during the jury selection process, known as 'voir dire' many flat out tell the court they think Casey Anthony killed Caylee. A few jurors even look straight at Casey with daggers in their eyes and a nervousness in their voice and say "I think she's guilty." There is a second of complete silence, a heaviness in the courtroom, every time one of the potential jurors utters these four words. Many of these potentials look really uncomfortable and are literally looking for the exit door. I get a sense they don't even want to be sitting here in the same room with Casey Anthony. The goal is to weed these people out and folks who haven't formed an opinion or find a few who have been living under a rock who haven't heard about the case. And guess what ? Amazingly they manage to find one or two who literally know nothing about it. Maybe I overindulge in watching news, but these people know 'nothing' about it ? I question their intellect, Can they think ? Are they aware of their surroundings? The Casey Anthony Case has been in the newspaper, on television and radio here in Florida for three years around the clock. You cannot go into a restaurant, bar or gas station which has a television on and not see something about the case. This change of venue, picking people from Pinellas County, will turn out to be the key in tipping the scale in favor of Casey being found not guilty. Walk around, interview the locals, and you will definitely find a lower socioeconomic element of

103

folks than they would've gotten in Orange County. The folks I talk too here seem a lot more liberal and a lot less judgmental. Judge Perry's two weeks of the reserved courtroom are almost up and he threatens to go next door to find jurors at a homeless shelter. So I go next door to do some reporting and I interview some of the homeless men who tell me there are TV's in the recreation rooms. Every homeless guy I speak too, knows who Casey Anthony is. And just because these men are down on their luck doesn't mean they can't sit and potentially serve on a jury in the sunshine state. Unlike in some places where the jury pool is picked from 'registered voters,' in Florida all you need to sit on a jury is a driver's license." It's widely known registered voters' are more educated, watch more news, and are therefore much more well informed."   **– Robyn Walensky**

"I think the jury from the OJ Simpson trial retired and moved to Florida."   **– Jay Leno on The Tonight Show**

"The point of picking in Pinellas was to find jurors who didn't have a bias toward the case and were not following it in the news. On day one, newspapers are being sold at three stands right outside the Criminal Justice Center. On day two, I come to the building and find someone taped up signs over the newspaper stands so potential jurors cannot read the headlines. In the end it won't matter, as a few of these potential jurors have probably never read a newspaper in their entire life. During the trial my suspicions about the raw intellect and intellectual curiosity of some of the jurors is confirmed as I stare at them daily from seat #1. At first blush I am amazed that some of the jurors aren't taking one note. But then my mind instantly flashes back to the jury selection process and I am reminded of some of their answers to the questions and I am actually not surprised about the lack of note taking and ability to focus. The defense got lucky. Theories that would be dismissed out-of-the-gate like the pool drowning are seeds of doubt that become imbedded in the minds of this crowd from Pinellas."   **– Robyn Walensky**

Newspaper Stands are covered outside the Pinellas County Justice Center on day #2 of Jury Selection

Photo Courtesy: Robyn Walensky

"At the end of this case , at the end of this case when you go back home, and you're back in Clearwater and you're sitting around the dinner table and someone say to you, "Why did you find Casey Anthony not guilty?" You're gonna say, well, I was fed a wealth of information, all this information came and it all boiled down to one thing. They couldn't tell me how she died. They couldn't prove this was a murder. They couldn't prove this was a manslaughter case. There was no evidence of any child abuse, and that's why we voted not guilty." **– Jose Baez during his opening statement**

CHAPTER 20

NOT GUILTY

"While everyone will be watching Casey, only the twelve jurors sit in judgment. I'm Robyn Walensky outside the courthouse. All of the breaking details NEXT in just ten minutes."
– Robyn Walensky in a news tease on WDBO radio – day one of the Casey Anthony trial

Orange County Protestor upset with Verdict outside Courthouse
Photo Courtesy: Robyn Walensky

"It's July 5, 2011. There is no justice for Caylee Marie Anthony. The world watches—— but like I say on day one of the trial, her fate is in the hands of twelve people. After a six-week trial, after less than eleven hours, the jury comes back with not guilty verdicts on all of the serious counts: first-degree murder, aggravated child abuse, aggravated manslaughter of a child. Casey Anthony is only found guilty on the four counts of lying to law enforcement. When I hear the words 'Not Guilty' being read out loud, I think I am dreaming. My immediate thought is, 'Did these jurors sit through the same trial I did?' 'Not Guilty,' 'Not Guilty,' 'Not Guilty.' I'm mentally and physically exhausted, so I still think I must be hearing it wrong. I feel like I watched a totally different TV show and they are weighing in on another program on another channel. Casey Anthony, a MOTHER, does NOT report her child missing for thirty-one DAYS? Isn't this child abuse? I can barely process in my brain what my ears are hearing. 'Not Guilty,' 'Not Guilty,' 'Not Guilty.' Absolutely unbelievable to me. And as I say on WDBO, the verdict is 'simply stunning. I feel like I watched a totally different trial.'" **– Robyn Walensky**

"How can you punish someone for something if you don't know what they did?"
– Juror #3, Jennifer Ford, thirty-two years old, nursing student, in an exclusive interview with ABC's Terry Moran on Nightline

"When I listen to juror # 3 speak out, I start to see how these Pinellas people come to their NOT Guilty verdicts. They wanted the prosecutors to play 'connect the dots' for them. Literally draw them a picture or, in this case, show them the video of the killer chloroforming Caylee with a rag, wrapping duct tape around her head, placing the heart-shaped sticker on the duct tape over her mouth, then putting her in a laundry bag and in two garbage bags and tossing her like trash into the woods. There is no video of this. The cause of death is a major stumbling block for jurors. In fact, juror #3 tells ABC's Terry Moran the first vote was 10-2 for NOT guilty on first degree murder." So the bottom line is the jurors believed the prosecution could not prove to them 'beyond a reasonable doubt' what the cause of death was." **– Robyn Walensky**

"There wasn't enough evidence. There wasn't anything strong enough to say, exactly. I don't think anyone in America could tell us exactly how she died. If you put even just the twelve jurors in one room with a piece of paper to write down how Caylee died, nobody knows. We'd all be guessing. We have no idea."

"I remember juror #1055 aka juror #3 from Pinellas…from my notes, she barely knew about the case and had little interest in it. I can understand being a student in a nursing program and not caring about some sensational story on TV, but for the life of me, how could you live in Florida and not know anything about this crime unless you're living under a rock? I also clearly recall juror #11. He's young nice-looking gym teacher studying for a master's degree online. He tells the court he watches very little TV and never watches Nancy Grace. He's clearly out of the Nancy Grace target demo being male and in his thirties. As for his position on the death penalty, 'I guess I could consider it, but having to make that decision would be very tough for me.' I remember thinking, the prosecutors are going to have real problems convincing these Pinellas people."

– Robyn Walensky

"Do you see that picture? Ha, I have no idea. They didn't even paint a picture for me to consider."

– Juror #3, Jennifer Ford, in an exclusive interview with ABC's Terry Moran on Nightline

"The state maintains it was PRE-meditated murder, that Casey researched how to make chloroform on the Anthony family computer."

– Robyn Walensky

"With the chloroform, I'm all over the place…I have no idea, I'm in a maze, I don't know where I'm at…I don't know where the end is. I'm not even quite sure where I began with the chloroform, so I can't get from beginning to end, A to B to C, what even happened…I can't make it work."

– Juror #3 Jennifer Ford, in an exclusive interview with ABC's Terry Moran on Nightline

"As for the thirty-one days Casey is running around Orlando, hanging with her boyfriend, partying, and getting a tattoo, the jurors shockingly don't buy into Casey's behavior."   **– Robyn Walensky**

"It looks very bad. The behavior is very bad. But, bad behavior is not enough to prove a crime. It's not."
– Juror #3, Jennifer Ford, in an exclusive interview with ABC's Terry Moran on Nightline

"Prosecutors say Casey killed Caylee, drove around with her body in the trunk of her car for a few days, then, when she was unable to bury her in the backyard with a neighbor's shovel, she dumps the already decomposing body in the woods around the corner from her house where she buried pets as a child. The problem though is because of Casey's initial lies that her daughter is kidnapped by Zanny the nanny, the wild goose chase at Universal Studios, time wasted on nonsense, the body is not found in a timely manner. Roy Kronk thinks he sees something and a sheriff's deputy is called to the woods scene but doesn't take him seriously and never searches the area. This deputy is fired. More time goes by. A storm rolls in to Central Florida. Caylee's body is decomposing in a muddy swamp under water. DNA and fingerprints are washing away. Unlike CSI, the TV show, there will be no forensic evidence to tie up at the end of the trial with a neat little red bow on it. Instead, jurors will buy into Jose Baez's theory that it was 'an accident that snowballed out of control.' That's easier on their brains to absorb than to add one plus one, which clearly equals two in this case."   **– Robyn Walensky**

"How did she die? If you are going to charge someone with murder don't you have to know how they killed someone ? Or why they might have killed someone? Or have something—where, when, why, how? Those are important questions. They were NOT answered." "I'm still confused. I still have no idea what happened to that child… I'm going to sleep just fine. Because in this country that's our Constitution. I applied the law. I did the best I could. I tried to make it work. I was reaching. 'Not guilty'—doesn't mean innocent…It doesn't feel good. It was a horrible decision to have to make. But I had to do it based on the law."

– Juror #3, Jennifer Ford, in an exclusive interview with ABC's Terry Moran on Nightline

"The only outstanding question I have in my mind…is why in the world didn't the state take these jurors on a field trip to see the swamp scene. I've been there after it rains, standing in the thick mud, smelling the moldy vines, foliage, weeds, and brush, and being bitten by the bugs; it has enormous impact. This is the furthest cry from the comfort of a two-year-olds Winnie the Pooh-decorated bedroom. Honestly it's one of the most horrible places on earth. And the twelve jurors never got to see it up close. A lot of their 'outstanding questions,' would have clearly been answered. There would be no doubt. This is the place where the baby girl, duct tape wrapped around her head, is rotting in all kinds of harsh weather in the woods. I make this point on the radio and on television." **– Robyn Walensky**

"On July 21, Nancy Grace lists the 'five pieces of missing evidence that could have nailed tot mom' that are kept from the jury, including a jailhouse video showing Casey's collapse when she finds out where cops are searching for Caylee's body, an allegation Casey wanted to put Caylee up for adoption, a furious fight with her mother, Cindy, the night before Caylee disappears, a so-called confession found in her diary, and testimony from two snitches who claim Casey had used chloroform on Caylee. Nancy asks me to comment."

– Robyn Walensky

"Nancy, the five things you just stated are key. In my opinion, the number one thing they should have done was taken the jurors to the Caylee crime scene, to see where the remains were recovered."

– Robyn Walensky on HLN's Nancy Grace, July 21, 2011

CHAPTER 21

THE COURT OF PUBLIC OPINION

"As soon as the not guilty verdict comes down, I head straight to the back of the Orange County Courthouse to get sound of the key figures from the trial leaving the building. The media has this area all staked out. There are wall-to-wall journalists drooling for video, sound bites and snapshots. I see CSI Geraldo Bloise leave with a disgusted look on his face. He refuses to speak into my tape recorder, but I am able to grab a picture of him on my BlackBerry. The look of disgust on his face speaks louder than his words could in this moment in time.

OCSO CSI Geraldo Bloise leaves court after Not Guilty Verdict
Photo Courtesy: Robyn Walensky

I realize this is going to be what I call 'sound bite light' so I call my bosses and I decide to hightail it down to Clearwater, one hundred miles, where this saga starts seven weeks ago. The goal is to track down the jurors for interviews as they return home. The media waits, but the twelve plus five alternates never return to the criminal justice center that night. This is a sampling of post-verdict comments I collect in the immediate aftermath from folks hanging out around the facility for my radio reports at WDBO." **– Robyn Walensky**

"WDBO anchor Bob Hazen tosses to me in a live report and I go on-air. "Bob—No sign of the jurors here in their home county. They are most likely off to New York for network TV interviews and to sign book deals. It was just six weeks ago the jurors were selected here in Pinellas County. Last night as we waited for jurors to arrive back home—which they did not. I spoke with folks here outside the criminal justice center—many looking visibly disgusted. Hillary Baldwin from St. Petersburg, Florida—her reaction."

– Robyn Walensky in WDBO radio report, the morning after the Casey Anthony verdict, reporting live from Clearwater, Florida

"She should have went to prison for life for that, there is no reason why she should be out, that poor little girl died for nothing."

– Hillary Baldwin, Pinellas County Resident

"The jury was picked here six weeks ago. What do you make of the jurors' decision?"

**– Robyn Walensky in an interview with.
Hillary Baldwin, Pinellas County resident**

"They are in Florida. They should know the whole thing about this, she's guilty, completely guilty she should get life. And there is no reason for her be out and running around with everybody. She is going to get knocked up again and the same thing is going to happen again to the next one."

– Pinellas County resident

"I think it's horrible. I think she should have been found guilty. I think the state proved their case well and I was shocked and I think the deliberation for what, a little over ten hours I think, they should have focused more on the evidence and what the state had."

– Barbie Harmon, Pinellas County resident

"Everybody was hoping that it actually went the other way. I was at the gym and everybody was glued to the TV. They were just waiting for 2:15, waiting to hear what was going to happen, the outcome, and everybody was shocked to find out that she was 'not guilty.' I believe that they did the best they could with the information they received. I don't think they had sufficient time to actually really make the right decision."

– Ramon Ortiz, Pinellas County resident

"Next up. It's sentencing day and Judge Perry speaks to the court."

– Robyn Walensky

"Do you realize that there are folks out there that want to do crazy things like filet open someone—pour salt on that person—and feed their legs to a piranha?"
– Judge Belvin Perry, Jr.

"I think our intelligence section is assessing the threats. Obviously some people have strong sentiments about the outcome. Once again, certainly no one has the right to take the law into their own hands. For us, Casey had her day in court, the prosecutors presented a case, the defense presented a case and the jury made a decision; they reached a verdict. I would hope people would kind of step back and regardless of their feelings, would not go out and commit another crime."
– Sergeant John Allen

Orange County Protestor upset with Verdict outside Courthouse
Photo Courtesy: Robyn Walensky

"Judge Perry sentences Casey Anthony on the four charges of lying to police. But because of 'time served,' Casey will be let out of jail in a matter of days. Outside, in front of the Orange County Courthouse, protestors against the verdict and those in support of it fill the two separated designated areas. People bring signs and they are angry. One lady shouts, "Connect the dots and it fits together like a puzzle. Casey Anthony killed her daughter and we let her go free.' Another woman with a sign that reads, "Jury NO BALLS." She shouts, 'She waited until she was born and then she aborted her life, it makes no difference.'" **– Robyn Walensky**

"My sign says, 'Arrest the Jury NO BALLS—No justice for Caylee.' We had twelve jurors where Floridians paid their tax money for justice, and we did not receive it. We did not get justice. And they sit up there and then they walked out with their smug faces and they exited because they knew there was no justice and now they are wanting six figures for interviews. It's blood money and we detest it and we are out here to show Caylee that we will stand up for her because no one will ever be accountable for her death and that is a miscarriage of justice."
– Protestor with "Jury NO BALLS" sign outside Orange County Courthouse on Casey sentencing day

"My sign says 'Casey Anthony, will you marry me?' And I'm here because I want to support Casey and give her a second chance."
– Young man who supports Casey Anthony outside Orange County Courthouse on Casey sentencing day

Orange County man happy with Verdict outside Courthouse
Photo Courtesy: Robyn Walensky

"How old are you and what do you do for a living?" **– Robyn Walensky**

"I'm twenty-four and I make pizzas."
– Young man who supports Casey Anthony

"So you want to date her and marry her?" **– Robyn Walensky**

"Eventually, yes." **– Young man who supports Casey Anthony**

"Why be mad at me? The prosecution had to prove it. Why is it my fault they didn't prove their case? If you give me the evidence I am happy to return a verdict accordingly, but if it's just not there I'm not going to speculate. I'm not going to be emotional and just charge somebody, I can't do that in good conscience...It's someone else's life in your hands so if they want to charge and they want me to take someone's life, they have to prove it, they have to prove it, or else I am a murderer too and I'm not any better."

**– Juror #3, Jennifer Ford, in an exclusive interview
with ABC's Terry Moran on Nightline**

"When I had to sign off on the verdicts, the sheet that given to me, there was just a feeling of disgust that came across me, knowing that my signature and her signature were going to be there on the same sheet."

**– Juror #11, the foreman, in exclusive interview with
Fox's Greta Van Susteren, On the Record**

"People have no reservation or hesitation about walking up to an individual pulling a gun, a knife, or any other type of weapon and because they disagree with them, uh, hurt them or kill them…the best that I think I can do—legally, is a cooling-off period. And at the conclusion of that cooling-off period, release the names."

**– Judge Belvin Perry, Jr., speaks to the court and decides
to release jurors' names at a later date**

CHAPTER 22

THE FIRST AND FINAL NEWS CONFERENCE

"Looming large in the second-floor conference room is a color photograph of a very innocent-looking Caylee Anthony. The picture is propped up on an easel and placed next to the row of chairs where seven seasoned detectives and CSIs who testified at trial answer a never-ending flow of questions from members of the media for an unprecedented ninety minutes. A week after the stunning not-guilty verdict, the Orange County Sheriff's Office decides to hold what I call on WDBO Radio 'a first and final news conference.' An opportunity for detectives and CSIs to speak out publicly for the first and final time." — **Robyn Walensky**

"We gave it 100 percent of our effort, trying to locate her. And to bring to justice the individuals who were responsible for this case." — **Sheriff Jerry Demings**

"It's still amazing to me how she (Casey) reacted, or how she didn't react inside the interview (at Universal Studios)." — **Corporal Yuri Melich**

"Ya know, I think it's been said by some people that we were desperate, when, in fact, we were desperate. We were desperate to find a child that we were told was missing." — **Sergeant John Allen**

"She (Casey) wouldn't tell us the truth and that's all we were after was the truth. That day, this whole thing could have ended had we known the truth."
– Corporal Yuri Melich

"It's the defense's job to cast doubt on the evidence we present. They called it fraud. I would have to disagree."
– Sandra Osborne, Orange County Sheriff's Office computer technician

"The cutting-edge forensic science explored in this case, like the collection of air samples to determine whether a decompositional event has taken place will hopefully become standard operating procedure in crime scene investigations across the county. The work we do, not only in this case, but in every case we do, has to be done methodically, precisely, and carefully. Because, if what we do is not done right, we can put an innocent person in jail for life, or let a guilty person go free."
– Crime Scene Supervisor Michael Vincent

"In our mind, George was never a suspect—our initial suspect in this was 'Zanny the nanny,' because that's what we were told. After the initial Zanny the nanny story, we followed the evidence. This case is really no different than any other case in this regard. We don't get to pick our witnesses. We don't pick who we ultimately interview. And part of our job is to sort through what people tell us to try to determine the truth, and it is not uncommon in any case for us to interview people who are not entirely truthful."
– Sergeant John Allen

"Those two parents, the grandparents, they were struggling with the fact that the more they assisted us, the more they helped us build the case with her."
– Detective Eric Edwards

"They wanted to find the child but I think they knew—well, I don't think they know specifics, what happened, but they got that car. I think they had a pretty good idea that something had occurred. They were struggling with the realization that the more they dealt with us and were interviewed by us the more solid our case became."
– Sergeant John Allen

"Detective Edwards and Detective Allen are pressed again on whether George Anthony was ever considered a suspect." **– Robyn Walensky**

"No." **– Detective Eric Edwards**

"The questions continue." **– Robyn Walensky**

"I think for me, obviously when we started this investigation, our initial interview with Casey—Yuri's initial interview, and then our follow-up interview when she took us out to Universal—we covered a lot of this. We asked whether or not this was a result of an accident. We did go down that road with her but everybody insisted that she'd been kidnapped by 'Zanny the nanny.' Obviously, what followed was an enormous search, like the sheriff mentioned. Early on, you know, we got six thousand leads in an eight-month time span. Obviously, we had to prioritize those leads because we were being told there was a live child out there who'd been kidnapped by a nanny. Obviously, the leads that took precedence were the live sightings. Fortunately for us, we had other agencies which were willing to help out and we were able to take the leads where somebody reported seeing her in other states and turned those over to the FBI. Well, they, in turn, sent agents out in those jurisdictions to follow up on those leads. The leads that came in out of state, where there was some urgency or some immediate filed data, we contacted police agencies across the country and asked them to go check these sightings, and then, of course, the Florida Department of Law Enforcement, they were following up on leads out of the local area and we had at any one given time, dozens of people here following up on live sights."

– Sergeant John Allen

"It is crystal clear to me these detectives went to work every day to do a job. It's also painfully obvious by how uncomfortable some of them look sitting up there on the stage, under the bright light, taking endless questions from the media, that the majority hate being in the spotlight. They are fact finders not showmen. Deputy Forgey, for example, who I do not know personally, seems shy. The detectives who sit at the podium are asked by a reporter at the news conference if their professional lives have changed now that they're 'household' names."   **– Robyn Walensky**

"It hasn't, except I get teased at work about it."**– Deputy Jason Forgey**

"Like what? Like what?"   **– Robyn Walensky**

"Saw you on TV again.' The typical stuff."   **– Deputy Jason Forgey**

"How about Gerus?"   **– Reporter at OCSO news conference**

"He's not doing any interviews. He's at home. He's enjoying what's left. In a little bit of pain but he's a great house dog."
– Deputy Jason Forgey

"Are you retiring him?"   **– Robyn Walensky**

"He's been retired."   **– Deputy Jason Forgey**

"He's been retired?"   **– Robyn Walensky**

"Yes. He came down with spondylosis. We didn't know until he actually went down on a call from pinching the nerves and everything and then they next day they x-rayed him, he was retired."
– Deputy Jason Forgey

"I'd like to say it hasn't changed at all. We all sit up here, we all have other cases to work. We've all worked other cases in the past three years. If anyone has said this has been our only case, then they'd be lying because we've all worked other cases. Every single one of them deserve the same attention that this has deserved, in my eyes. So as far as professionally, no, this hasn't changed. Although now when I show up, people tend to recognize me, where I wish they hadn't."
– Corporal Yuri Melich

"For me, it was just very time consuming. Like I said before, with over six thousand leads coming in, we were very, very busy for a significant amount of time. I'm a husband and a father. I've got a family at home.

So I guess the most significant thing for me was, because it was so time consuming, I spent less time with my family. It's over. We each— Eric, Yuri and I—we've all gone to different assignments. And like the sheriff said, we're moving on to other things, other cases."

– Sergeant John Allen

"I would say it hasn't changed that much. We still—all of us in the forensic unit—we still work as hard on any crime scene that we did on this case and I'd say the only difference is that now witnesses will actually recognize me on a crime scene but that's about the only difference."

– CSI Jennifer Welch

"I agree with my co-worker. The same thing."

– Geraldo Bloise

"I'd like to say mine hasn't changed but it has. I've learned a lot through the case of this investigation. I was very new in 2008 when this started. I had been doing computer forensics for about a year. It was my first homicide case. What a way to start. So I thought, you know, let's just jump in and do it and learn as much as I can. I've done that. I've increased my training. I think my skills have gotten better. . I've learned a lot. The buzz around the computer forensics community, of course is this case right now. What we did, what we didn't do, what we could've done better. I have requests for all kinds of logs and interviews and things like that for our unit. Of course we're not going to do too much in reference to the case specifically but it's been good for training. It's been good for computer forensic examiners to see what exactly the questions are that are asked on the stand, how to perform on the stand. A lot of computer forensic examiners are new, like myself. We haven't had a whole lot of experience testifying as to our craft yet. So we're going to use this as much as we can for training and for the experience of it. And we're just going to keep moving forward and we'll learn everything that we can."

– Orange County Sheriff's Office Computer Technician Sandy Osborne

"Again, it goes back. We have to respect our judicial system. We have to respect what a jury is brought to a courtroom to do. Whether we agree with it or disagree with it. I can tell you obviously I'm unhappy that it's a different verdict. I felt strongly in the case and I still do. But as far as bringing closure to people, people just have to understand this is our judicial system. We have to have faith in it. We have to rely on it. We can't simply have our own belief and outcome on what it should be and disregard what the Constitution has provided us. I wish there was something I could say that would bring closure to everyone but there isn't. I just know that unfortunately people are going to have to come to their own sense of closure within themselves and know that as far as this case is concerned, as far as the judicial system is concerned on this, there's nothing else that we can do."

– Corporal Yuri Melich

"I certainly don't have any doubt. We worked very hard on this case. I think all of us respect the jury system and respect the jury's verdict. I would hope that people who followed this, people in the community, would also respect the jury's verdict and our process. But for us, I certainly don't have any doubt after working on this. I felt our case was solid."

– Sergeant John Allen

"Obviously, I feel, I still feel, felt strongly on this case. If we didn't feel strong on it we wouldn't have brought it to the grand jury. We wouldn't have proceeded the way we felt. And I echo Sergeant Allen's sentiments of the jury. You know, ultimately it's up to the jury to decide. We respect that and we honor that. We feel very confident and I'm extremely grateful for the people who helped work this case. People in this agency, their caliber is just bar none. They are some of the best people you could have working on a case. Our crime scene investigators, our computer forensic examiners, they are just stellar. I wish I could go into all these stories on how great they are. But yeah, we feel confident, still feel confident. My wife is happy is happy it's over. It's a case. Unfortunately, yes, it did take three years of our lives, because anyone here, including those who aren't on camera, dedicated themselves, dedicated three years to this. We just have to move on. There are other cases to work. There are other victims out there who are going to need our help and hopefully we're going to be able to help them."

– Corporal Yuri Melich

"I want to go back to the CSI and the forensics…were you disappointed—either of one of you—that the canisters that were collected of the actual smell, that there was a decision made by the judge that the jurors were never going to smell the smell, and that the jurors were not actually taken on a field trip out to that crime scene? Do either one of you want to address those questions about the smell in the canisters and no field trip out to the swamp?"
– Robyn Walensky during OCSO news conference
during Q and A with CSIs Welch and Bloise

"Regarding to the canister, I respect the decision of the court. I respect the judge's decision."   **– CSI Geraldo Bloise**

"But do you think that it would have impacted the jurors if they would have actually been able to smell the smell?"   **– Robyn Walensky**

"Yes." – CSI Geraldo Bloise

"And taking them out on a trip there to the swamp?"
– Robyn Walensky

"I can't say if it would've helped or not. I mean, obviously, it looks a lot different than the very first day we were out there. So I don't know if that would have impacted or not."   **– CSI Jennifer Welch**

"I really thought that it was important that we give our community, and really the nation, the opportunity to have some closure, if you will, as it relates to this investigation. But the ones who have joined us this afternoon are individuals who played principal roles in the investigation. They have volunteered to come here this afternoon and just to tell you a little bit about this case. On July 15, 2008, at approximately 8:00 p.m., the Orange County Sheriff's Office received its first 9-1-1 call for a missing toddler by the name of Caylee Marie Anthony. Little did we know, it would become the Casey Anthony case that would dominate our time and resources for several years. Here are a few facts that we were able ascertain as it relates to the man hours and other resources that were committed to this case.

There were 6,165 tips that were received by the missing persons squad during an eight-month period of time. More than one hundred FBI agents followed up on the state leads. More than forty Florida Department of Law Enforcement agents followed up on state leads that emanated out of this local area. The Orange County Sheriff's Office personnel followed up countless leads throughout the investigation. The Metropolitan Bureau of Investigation dealt with many of the technical aspects of the investigation. We received assistance from the Osceola County Sheriff's Office. We received assistance from the Orlando Police Department, the Orange County Medical Examiner's Office, all the local law enforcement agencies and of course, the state attorney's office here from the ninth judicial circuit. The Orange County forensics personnel collected more than six hundred pieces of evidence. The FBI lab handled nearly five hundred pieces of that evidence. This is a wonderful example of the partnership and collaboration between multiple agencies who worked very well together for a common good. The community came out and assisted in the search for a missing child. We have thanked our community for their assistance in this process, as well."

– Sheriff Jerry Demings

"The formal portion of the news conference ends. Now it's time for the rapid fire question. I raise my hand and Captain Angelo Nieves, the PIO, or public information officer, calls on me. I literally have a million questions running through my mind, but I will really narrow it down."

– Robyn Walensky

"Two questions. One for the sheriff and one for the CSIs. First to the sheriff. I'm struck by the photograph here in the room of Caylee. If you could address the significance."

– Robyn Walensky

"Well, the reason we have the photograph here today is really simple. That is what this was all about. It was about a missing child, a two-and-a-half-year-old, and that is really what motivated our staff, our community to have the concerns that they have so that dominates the case. It was really about her."

– Sheriff Jerry Demings

"Then, my follow-up."   **– Robyn Walensky**

"And when you look over at this and you see her face and what she was reduced to, how does that make you feel?"   **– Robyn Walensky**

Sheriff Demings pauses. "Well, I can tell you this, as a father, as a grandfather, I have a three-year-old granddaughter. It's disturbing to me. I wouldn't wish what happened to her on any parent and so we responded to that. We gave it a hundred percent of our effort trying to locate her and to bring to justice the individuals who were responsible in this case."   **– Sheriff Jerry Demings**

"One of the things I wanted to make sure people understood is that we thank the community and we thank the people who have followed this case, who have sent us letters, who have sent us e-mails, who have made phone calls, who have sent flowers to not only the sheriff's office, the CSI personnel, but also the state attorney's office. These people who went through these efforts, took time out of their lives to say 'thank you' or 'job well done.' We thank them so very much because those words of encouragement—to me, personally—meant a lot so if there's any chance in thanking these people, I would really like to share my thanks, personally, and thanks to the sheriff's office. I went to Publix two days ago. I had lady with a shopping cart come up to me, shake my hand, and said, 'Thank you. Job well done.' I had the lady behind the counter, who was making my sub, say, 'Thank you. Job well done.' I'm not used to the attention. You become a cop to get the bad guy. You make sure the victim has justice. You don't go to be a celebrity or something. I'm not used to it. I feel very awkward about it."
    – Corporal Yuri Melich in an interview with Robyn Walensky

"Well, we're planning for whatever the outcome will be but I believe that history has clearly demonstrated that this community will maintain a peaceful resolve in this situation, so we have nothing to indicate otherwise, when she is released this weekend. As it relates to our protection or security of Casey Anthony—that will conclude when she's released from custody and she becomes a citizen. However, if she maintains her housing here in our jurisdiction, if we become aware of any threats—any credible threats—to her, she is like every other resident or citizen here. We have an obligation to protect and provide for her safety and security. If she moves on to some other location, then that becomes someone else's responsibility at that point. So we just don't know, but we will not be providing any elaborate security or protection for Casey once she leaves. There has been a plethora of chatter in the social media circles where people have expressed their displeasure over the verdict and their displeasure with her. But as of today, we don't have credible threats to move forward. Any type of active prosecution, if you will, in that case. We will just see what the future brings in that regard. Corrections is responsible for their inmate and as long as she is in their custody and inside the Orange County Jail as an inmate, they have the responsibility for her safety and security. Once she leaves the grounds of the Orange County Jail and she's a free citizen, at that point, the only thing that we would do is facilitate that departure. It is unknown where she's going to land after she leaves from the Orange County Jail and we don't pick up any security responsibility again unless there's some type of credible threat. So once she leaves that property, she's no longer the responsibility, from a security protective need, of either Corrections or the Orange County Sheriff's Office. We will assist in her departure from that property, from those premises. After that, unless there's some other reason for us to be involved with her, we will not be involved with her. If there's some public safety—some overriding public safety—need for us to because of the cost of traffic or whatever, then we'll have to do our jobs in that case, but we're not going to be her personal security. Her attorneys will make appropriate decisions and prepare for her own security after that. That will not be our responsibility. We give every crime victim appropriate attention. If we have another high-profile case, another case involving a child like this, who cannot stand and speak for herself, you can believe we are going to bring to bear the resources—the full resources—of the Orange County Sheriff's Office and all those other agencies that assisted in this case, as well. So, the nature of each case kind of dictates the response that you get. We'll respond appropriately. Again I do thank you all for coming. Hopefully, this has been fruitful for you and we have responded very candidly to your questions. Again, I ask your patience and understanding as we move forward in the future when we say that these individuals are not available, they are going to focusing on the work and as some may have indicated, we have other crime victims we have to take care of, as well, in the process. So, again, thank you all very much." **– Sherriff Jerry Demings**

"Certainly it's not uncommon when we investigate a murder for people to lie to us. I think we're all used to dealing with that. I think probably the frustrating thing about these particular lies would be that for such a long time, because of the large volume of information that came in and the extensive search, the resources that were used, that were used to search for her not only here in Orange County by the Sheriff's Office, but throughout the state, by the Florida Department of Law Enforcement and across the country by the FBI and other agencies that were looking for a live child based on what we were told. These were all resources that the taxpayers ultimately funded and were resources that could have been used to find other missing children who were missing. That—at least I think for me personally—is probably the most frustrating." **– Sergeant John Allen**

"I think that ultimately our agency did a very, very good job, a very, very thorough job investigating this case. I'm proud of working for the agency. I'm very proud of the people I work for and I work with. The CSIs are just phenomenal. I hope that someday they get the recognition they deserve for working so hard and so diligently on this. I think we did everything we could." **– Corporal Yuri Melich**

"When you have a child, that child becomes your life. This case is about the clash between that responsibility, and the expectations that go with it, and the life that Casey Anthony wanted to have."
– Jeff Ashton during his closing argument

"As difficult as it may be to accept that any mother would intentionally kill her own child, from the evidence that you will hear in this case, there is no other conclusion that can be drawn. Caylee Marie Anthony was not kidnapped by a nanny, or any other person. No

one but Casey Anthony had access to all the pieces of evidence in this case. The duct tape, the laundry bag, the blanket, the shorts, the shirt, the car. No one else lied to their friends, to the family, to investigators. No one else benefited from the death of Caylee Marie Anthony. Caylee's death allowed Casey Anthony to live the good life. At least for those thirty-one days.
– Linda Drane Burdick during her opening argument

"The strategy behind that is, if you hate her, if you think she's a lying, no-good slut, then you'll start to look at this evidence in a different light. I told you at the very beginning of this case that this was an accident that snowballed out of control...What made it unique is not what happened, but who it happened to."
– Jose Baez during his closing argument

"So she has a choice—a life tethered to a child or a life free to be twenty-two...those were Casey's choices. The life that she wanted, or the life that she had. And as hard as it is for anyone to imagine she had to choose between sacrificing two things. The first was her dreams and the life that she wanted, second was her child. And we submit to you the evidence in this case shows, that the choice she made was her child."
– Prosecutor Jeff Ashton during his closing argument

"The burden rests on the shoulders of my colleagues at the state attorney's office." **– Defense attorney Cheney Mason**

"Was George Anthony's life better? Mr. Ashton went over what George Anthony's life was like as a result of losing his beloved granddaughter. Whose life was better? That's the only question you need to answer in considering why Caylee Marie Anthony was left on the side of the road dead. There's your answer."
– Prosecutor Linda Drane Burdick during her rebuttal closing argument.

"Burdick publishes a picture on the courtroom monitor. It's a split screen. On the left a close-up picture of Casey's 'Bella Vita' tattoo, on the right a picture of Casey dancing the night away. It's a dramatic and powerful close. In a super simple way, it speaks to motive. Premeditated murder. Casey plans to party and live the good life once her daughter is out of the picture. Burdick pauses, and wraps it up with four words."

– Robyn Walensky

"Thank you, Your Honor."

– Prosecutor Linda Drane Burdick's last words
of her rebuttal closing argument

On July 17, 2011, Casey Anthony is released from jail—just a few weeks before what would have been Caylee Marie Anthony's sixth birthday.

CHAPTER 23

TRIAL TAKEAWAYS

"People often ask me what I will remember most about the Casey Anthony trial. The most startling image: clearly the crime scene photos of Caylee's small skull covered with a mat of hair, lying on the ground with weeds growing through and around it. The weather-worn duct tape can be seen on the nose and mouth area holding her mandible, or jaw bone, together. A little girl should not end up like this. No one should ever end up like this. People don't treat their pets this way let alone an adorable innocent two-year-old. The sharp contrast of any picture the world has seen of a smiling vibrant healthy Caylee compared to the crime scene photo of her skull shown only in the courtroom is overwhelming. The pictures will be with me for the rest of my life. Casey can turn on the tears in court, then seconds later sit there like a statue, looking almost frozen. For a second she looks like a picture of a modern day Mona Lisa. She has a unique ability to go from first to fifth gear in literally an instant. All of us in court watched her turn on the waterworks and cry for the jury and look away from the TV monitor showing one of those pictures of her deceased daughter's skull, to laughing large with her lawyers. She can turn it on and off with the flip of a figurative switch. This woman in a word is, *insane*. I give her this. She's smarter than anyone in her family. She thought she was smarter than the seasoned detectives, some who have more than three decades of experience under their belts. And Casey Anthony is a great liar. The apple they say doesn't fall far from the tree. The world watched as both her mother and her father told many many mistruths. The state sees right through all the nonsense. And for me the most compelling portion of the trial that I will always remember is Linda Drane Burdick's opening argument; "Where is Caylee?" Her delivery is so powerful and it will always stick with me. She opens the case by meticulously and methodically going through each of the thirty-one days Caylee is missing, detailing day by day, hour by hour Casey's actions and lie after lie after lie. Burdick's carefully crafted words echo after every section, 'Where is Caylee? Where is Caylee?'" **– Robyn Walensky**

"So what happened? Day one, Monday June 16, 2008. Cell phone records for Casey Anthony showed that she did not leave the area of her parents' house until 4:00 p.m. that day, despite the fact that her father saw her leave the residence at 12:50. When she leaves, she tells her father, George, that she's going to spend the night with Caylee with a babysitter. She told her mother that she was going to spend the night with a babysitter by the name of Zanny. You will learn during the testimony and evidence in this case, there is no Zanny. Like Casey Anthony's job, Casey Anthony's babysitter was a figment of her imagination. So when Casey Anthony appears on a surveillance video at a Blockbuster with her boyfriend, Tony Lazzaro, on the night of June 16 of 2008 at 7:54 p.m., where is Caylee Anthony?"
– Prosecutor Linda Drane Burdick during her opening statement

"The most endearing picture of Caylee is the last picture of her ever taken. She's sitting on the lap of her great grandfather (Cindy's father) in a nursing home on Father's Day 2008." **– Robyn Walensky**

Last known photo of Caylee Anthony alive on Father's Day 2008

at nursing home with her Great Grandfather

"Florida State Attorney's Office, 9th Judicial Circuit"

"This isn't about Casey Anthony. It is about what happened between the photograph taken on Father's Day, June 15, 2008, and the photograph taken on December 11, 2008."

– Prosecutor Linda Drane Burdick during her opening statement

"And then there's that one two punch in the gut, the two words that sum up with a vivid image the absolute horror of this case...what Jeff Ashton calls "Caylee's coffin."
– Robyn Walensky

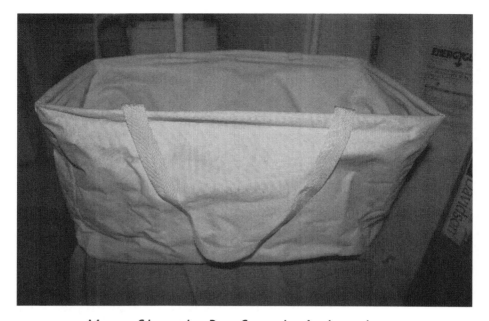

Mate of Laundry Bag from the Anthony home
"Florida State Attorney's Office, 9th Judicial Circuit"

"This was the bag that Caylee was found in, this is what, I guess you could say this was her coffin."
– Prosecutor Jeff Ashton during his closing argument

"Ashton shows another white laundry bag recovered from the Anthony home with the same "Whitney design" on it to the jury."
– Robyn Walensky

"This is the mate of the bag that served as Caylee's Coffin."
– Prosecutor Jeff Ashton during his closing argument

"The last outfit Caylee wore will also stick with me. The photographs of Caylee's tattered clothes recovered at the swamp scene shown in court, her little shorts and the letters from the logo on her T-shirt she had on that day: "Big trouble comes in small packages. Cindy claims she never liked this shirt. It was Casey who dressed Caylee in it on the morning she disappears."
– Robyn Walensky

"Most disturbing is the graphic sexual molestation allegations lobbied by Jose Baez against father George Anthony. At one point during this three-year odyssey, George attempts suicide. I come away believing he was distraught and wanted out forever. He's a retired police officer. Police officers are sworn to help you, and to get to the truth. George could not help Caylee. And he couldn't get to the truth with Casey either. What comes to mind is Linda Burdick's opening statement. And the feeling of helplessness George Anthony must still feel in his bones to this day as he thinks back to the last moment he saw Caylee alive."
                                                    – Robyn Walensky

"George Anthony specifically recalls that at 12:50 p.m. on June 16 in 2008, his daughter, Casey, left the residence on Hopespring Drive with Caylee Marie Anthony. Caylee was wearing a pink shirt, jean shorts, sunglasses and a backpack. And "JoJo," George Anthony, kissed his granddaughter good-bye. And never saw her again. In fact, no one but Casey Anthony ever saw Caylee Marie Anthony alive again. We've already shown you the last photographs taken of Caylee Anthony. The next time a photograph is taken of Caylee Anthony is on December 11 of 2008."
                    – Prosecutor Linda Drane Burdick during her opening
                                                            statement

"Other memorable moments at Trial. Prosecutor Jeff Ashton outlining Casey's compulsive lies. Linda Drane Burdick appropriately calls Casey a 'pathological liar.' And Ashton drives the ball home in dramatic fashion, with lots of repetition."   **– Robyn Walensky**

"On July 15, all hell breaks loose. July 15, the car is discovered, Cindy is on a mission. Cindy is on a mission. Cindy is going to find and see her granddaughter; she will not be denied and that's it. She tracks down Casey… grabs Casey, says, 'You will take me to my granddaughter NOW.' She (Casey) tries to rely on the old song, 'She's at Zanny's. I don't want to wake her up. She's at Zanny's, she's at Zanny's, she's at Zanny's'—despite everything that Cindy says, despite the threat of Cindy Anthony to call the police, she sticks to the story same old song: Zanny, Zanny, Zanny, Zanny, Zanny, Zanny."
                    – Prosecutor Jeff Ashton during his closing argument

"The most entertaining is defense witness is Dr. Werner Spitz, the famous forensic pathologist who reminds me of Dr. Henry Kissinger in looks, age, and accent. Despite how serious the subject matter is, Spitz is feisty and very entertaining to watch but really does not impact the outcome of the verdict. He's there to pour buckets of ice cold water on the State's case. Spitz, a witness for the defense, performed a second autopsy on Caylee and comes to court armed with a human skull. It sits with him on the witness stand during a Saturday session and when he first pulls it out there is sort of a stunned pause in the courtroom as people for a split second, including myself think, 'Wow, is that Caylee's skull?' But the skull is large and clearly that of an adult. Spitz has some miles clocked on his odometer. When he details his credentials he tells the court he was educated in Israel before it became a state and was still called Palestine. Spitz's takeaway point: he calls the autopsy done by medical examiner Dr. Jan Garavaglia 'shoddy' because she didn't open Caylee's skull. Dr. Spitz also claims someone may have 'staged' some of the crime scene photos. 'The person who took this picture, the person who prepared this, put the hair there.' On cross-examination, Jeff Ashton asks Spitz, 'So your testimony is the medical examiner's personnel took the hair that wasn't on the skull, placed it there?' Spitz answers, 'It wouldn't be the first time, sir. I can tell you some horror stories about that.'"
— **Robyn Walensky**

"What do you think about Dr. Spitz saying the photographers staged the skull and the hair at the crime scene?"
— **Robyn Walensky in an interview with CSI Jennifer Welch**

"Obviously, I heard about it after the trial was over and I'd have to say that it's totally false. I mean, we do the best job that we can and we would never ever stage anything at a crime scene. We document, photograph it, collect it as it is."
— **CSI Jennifer Welch**

"As far as the 'baby daddy.' At trial, we never learn who Caylee's father is; we do learn who is not. George and Lee Anthony are ruled

out through paternity tests. Casey is a compulsive liar who's had multiple partners. Various boyfriends are also ruled out through paternity tests. Casey tells a female inmate Caylee's father died in a car accident. The deceased boy's mother has been on TV and has provided photos of her son as a baby. I've seen the pictures and he looks just like Caylee. Perhaps he is the father. As of this writing, DNA testing has not yet been done."
– Robyn Walensky

"We never concluded who Caylee's father was. With respect to the sexual abuse allegations, the only thing that we have to indicate that there was any sexual abuse would be Casey's word."
– Sergeant John Allen during an OCSO news conference

"We had two prior boyfriends that provided their end information, if you will. Very vague. And then later down the road, there was something mentioned in a jailhouse letter. There was even less information. And I know as an agency or an investigative body, we sat down and discussed how to approach that if, in fact, we were going to look into in. And we did, in fact, reach out to the Baez law firm and were asked not to approach her at the jail. So for us to be able to build a platform to investigate that particular topic, we were never afforded that opportunity."
– Detective Eric Edwards

"The other outstanding question I have is why inmates who had contact with Casey behind bars are never called by the State to testify at trial. There is inmate Robyn Adams, who is currently serving time at the Federal Correctional Institute in Tallahassee, and inmate Maya Derkovic who is currently at the Lowell Correctional Institute in Ocala. Both women had contact with Casey Anthony behind bars in Orange County. Derkovic is in jail in 2008–2009 before being transferred to the lockup in Ocala. Corporal Yuri Melich receives a call from her and takes a sworn and recorded statement in December 2009. Derkovic tells OCSO detectives Casey tells her three different versions of how Caylee went missing, all involving the fictitious babysitter. That when Casey returned from the phone call visits with her parents she'd reportedly say derogatory things about her mother,

Cindy. 'At least the bitch knows how I feel now.' Derkovic claims Casey also told her she believed her mother loved Caylee more than she loved her. When Derkovic encourages Casey to tell the truth, Casey reportedly tells her she's not worried about doing the time and is only concerned with what people would think of her. Derkovic goes on to tell the detectives that after Casey sees herself on the news it is reportedly 'all fun and games to her. It was funny to her, it was exciting. When she found out she was going national, like it was national news now, to her it was like exciting.' Maya Derkovic also tells OCSO detectives Casey never mentions Caylee except when she makes comments to the tune of regretting having had a child."

– Robyn Walensky

"She just…never mentioned her. The only time she mentioned her was that maybe she should've waited to have a baby. Because she was young and she wanted to live life. Maybe she should never have had a baby before…a baby was stopping her from living life and partying. And a lot of times it interfered with having a boyfriend, having a child. And that's the only time she ever mentioned her baby."

– Inmate Maya Derkovic in a jailhouse interview with Corporal Yuri Melich December 11, 2009

"Derkovic goes on to describe the scene one day as Casey is being shackled before being led to go and speak with her lawyers. Inmates are shouting at her."

– Robyn Walensky

"People would yell through the door, 'Where's Caylee?' 'Where's Caylee?' 'Casey, where is Caylee?' And she'll laugh and smile as if it was nothing. She'll just start giggling and laughing. And ah, that right there shows that you really don't care. I mean they were trying to be nasty, but to her it was funny."

– Inmate Maya Derkovic in a jailhouse interview with Corporal Yuri Melich, December 11, 2009

"But the biggest bombshell is about 'knocking Caylee out."

– Robyn Walensky

"That she'll go out after Caylee went to sleep. That she'll sometimes knock her out and make her go to sleep until she came back."
– Inmate Maya Derkovic in a jailhouse interview with Corporal Yuri Melich, December 11, 2009

"The OCSO detectives ask Derkovic if Casey ever told her what she used to knock Caylee out with."   **– Robyn Walensky**

"No, but I assume it's drugs, because when someone says 'knock out,' it's drugs."
– Inmate Maya Derkovic in jailhouse interview with Corporal Yuri Melich, December 11, 2009

"It's February 12, 2010. FDLE (Florida Department of Law Enforcement investigators interview Robyn Adams who agrees to a sworn and recorded interview at the prison in Tallahassee where she's serving ten years on a drug conviction. During the interview, Adams tells detectives Casey told her Caylee had trouble sleeping and she had to use chloroform to put her to sleep. An investigator asks Adams about what Casey told her in a letter about the fictitious baby sitter, Zenaida."   **– Robyn Walensky**

"Zenaida wasn't, there was no Zenaida."
– Inmate Robyn Adams, February 12, 2010

"Adams goes on to tell the investigator about a conversation she has with Casey the night bones are found in an Orlando park."
– Robyn Walensky

"They found a bag of bones, and they were concerned that, um, that turned out to be bogus, and I waited and I talked to Casey that night and I told her kind of like how I would talk to anybody, dude they just found a bag of bones, I guess they found something in Blanchard Park and she kinda, her reaction to that was, 'It's not my daughter.'"
– Inmate Robyn Adams, February 12, 2010

"The detective presses Adams for her reaction to Casey's reaction."
– Robyn Walensky

"Um hmm, she kinda, she kinda, kinda, I mean it just sounds so harsh when I say this—she kinda giggled, in just…not in like an evil way, she just kind of like…it's not my kid, it's not my daughter. There was no…"   **– Inmate Robyn Adams, February 12, 2010**

"The investigator asks if she was taken aback, and did it make her look at Casey differently."   **– Robyn Walensky**

"Yeah. A little bit."   **– Inmate Robyn Adams, February 12, 2010**

"Adams also tells the investigators she spoke to Casey on the day Caylee's remains are found, December 11, 2008, after a chaplain informs Casey. The investigator grills Adams on specifically what Anthony told her about the find."   **– Robyn Walensky**

"They found remains and they found it in a bag, it was a black bag, garbage bag."   **– Inmate Robyn Adams, February 12, 2010**

"The investigator goes on—'OK, anything else? Anything else in the bag or—?'"   **– Robyn Walensky**

"There was a baby blanket."   **– Inmate Robyn Adams, February 12, 2010**

"BOMBSHELL…Casey knows. Even though these details of the blanket and bag have NOT been told to the jail chaplain. The bottom line, Casey has information only the cops, medical examiners, and the killer knows about. This is NEVER revealed at trial. The special investigator presses on, and Robyn Adams reveals that while Casey had no reaction when the bones were found in the park she is crying when she hears about the remains found down the street from her parents' house."   **– Robyn Walensky**

"She was crying and she was…she was scared. She was very scared. It was different from the Blanchard Park thing, yeah, very different… because her reaction was different. Her reaction was from Blanchard Park there wasn't any concern."
                    – Inmate Robyn Adams, February 12, 2010

"The investigator asks Adams, 'And what about this?'"
– Robyn Walensky

"Scared, tears."
– Inmate Robyn Adams to a detective, February 12, 2010

"The investigator goes on, 'At that point in time, in your heart of hearts did you know, you knew it was Caylee. Just by her reaction.'"
– Robyn Walensky

"Yes."   **– Inmate Robyn Adams to a detective, February 12, 2010**

"And there are more incredible revelations during the first prison interview with Robyn Adams. Turns out Adams claims she and Casey were allowed to spend time alone together thanks to the help of a corrections officer. No other inmates reportedly had these privileges. Adams claims she spent as much as four to five days per week with Anthony and the time frame—from minutes to hours. The contact reportedly ranged from speaking though the cell door to spending time in the same cell. Robyn Adams denies a sexual relationship with Casey Anthony or with the corrections officer who allowed the contact to occur. The corrections officer in question claims she allowed the women to have face-to-face contact at Anthony's cell door, but flat out denies allowing them to spend time together in the same cell. The corrections officer claims she allowed Adams to cut Anthony's hair on one occasion. It never ceases to amaze me that almost everyone associated with this trial is a flat-out liar."   **– Robyn Walensky**

"Robyn Adams says she's told about 75 to 80 percent of what she knows. And will spill the rest only when she has an attorney present. Investigators return on March 4, 2010 for a second follow-up sworn interview."   **– Robyn Walensky**

"Were there times when you actually were in the same cell together?"
– FDLE Special Agent Chris Woehr, investigator, asking Robyn Adams if she was ever alone in jail with Casey Anthony during a March 4, 2010, interview

"Yeah."**– Inmate Robyn Adams with attorney present, March 4, 2010**

"In her sworn statements, Adams flat out denies a sexual relationship with Casey or with the corrections guard that allowed this contact to happen." **– Robyn Walensky**

"And speaking of yet another jailhouse revelation, I learn through the state attorney's office documents Krystal Holloway's sister, Cecelia Benhaida, whose nickname is 'Sky,' also spent time in the Orange County Jail from August 21, 2008, until December 5, 2008, under the name Cecelia Holloway, and she too had contact with Casey Anthony. When Sky gets out, she learns of her sister's 'relationship' with George Anthony. She meets with the Anthony's, both Cindy and George, but claims not once did they ever ask her how Casey was doing behind bars." **– Robyn Walensky**

"The most arrogant person at this entire trial is Casey Anthony. Post trial when I get a minute to breathe, I spend hours poring through her jailhouse letters, more than 250 handwritten pages. She writes large and in script. Casey's letters go on and on and on. The ramblings of someone young. Love notes to another female inmate. There are quotes from the Bible. Quotes from books. Casey complains about noisy prisoners. Sometimes she rants about nothing. Oh and then her signature. She always signs her name with a heart next to it. Honestly, it's sickening. Every time I see the heart, my mind flashes to the heart-shaped sticker put on the duct tape over Caylee's mouth. And then there's this snippet. Which speaks for itself." **– Robyn Walensky**

"I haven't heard anything about my family today…on the radio… except talk of a Caylee tribute doll, and some hick from Louisiana selling three voodoo dolls on eBay. Guess who it's supposed to be? Jose told me last night he's already hired me another attorney to deal with those things. (Sigh) Another day, another series of rumors and ridiculousness. The life of a celebrity, huh? Right. If only I were old and ugly, then they wouldn't care. Sad that those words have come from people in the media, not just me. And I guess that stupid (bleep

bleep) Nancy Grace was on The View talking about me. Really? What a joke! Crazy bitch will have the lawsuit of a lifetime, really, only in hopes of getting her kicked off TV. Yes, I'm a bitch. Ya blame me? Nah." (Then there's a mean face Casey doodles on the paper.)

– Casey Anthony in a handwritten jailhouse letter

"The trial is shocking and sad. Compelling and captivating. There is worldwide interest. One little girl captures and keeps the attention of our entire country and the world…people tuned in for every development. I am reminded how far-reaching TV is, and how the Internet unites us in seconds. The most interesting thing that happens to me personally involves a postcard I pick up from the swamp scene and read on HLN's Nancy Grace show. There are hundreds of teddy bears, crosses, dolls, flowers, candles, and notes being left by strangers from all over the globe at the location. The rain taking a toll on some of the items. Magic marker on posters running, and notes of hope written in pen or pencil fading in the blazing summer sun. One night I randomly pick up a postcard that is about to sink into the thick mud. On it a picture of the city of Chicago. It's the kind of postcard one would pick up at the airport. And it turns out, this is exactly where it was bought."

– Robyn Walensky

"We are taking your calls. Standing by right now at Caylee's memorial site, Robyn Walensky, WDBO. Robyn, a lot of activity there. What's happening? Show me." **– HLN's Nancy Grace, July 18, 2011**

"Well, Nancy, there's so much going on here. Let's say that the folks that are coming out here to the scene are leaving all sorts of beautiful, beautiful flowers with little notes on them. I'm standing here in front of the beautiful cross, Caylee Marie. Someone, Nancy—remember, we heard so much about the little Winnie the Pooh blanket? Well, someone today put up the little Disney Winnie the Pooh book here. Someone left jelly beans.

I want to read you the note, Nancy. It says, 'Thinking of you, Caylee. Rest in peace, my little friend.' This is all the way from Scotland. And,

Nancy, I want to show you just how terrible this scene is. Walk with me, if you will, into the mud. I have boots on. You can hear—actually hear the sloshing. Whoever left this child here, whoever dumped this body in this scene never wanted little Caylee to be found again. It is so horrible out here, so hot, so buggy, so smelly. And here in the woods, people have put all sorts of little toys and stuffed animals. It is so sad. Her birthday would have been coming up in just a few weeks, Nancy, and that's why you see, you know, all these little balloons, 'It's all about you, 'Happy birthday, Caylee, August 9, 2011.'"

– Robyn Walensky on HLN's Nancy Grace, July 18, 2011

"The show continues with various other guests, but Nancy comes back to me for another live hit."   **– Robyn Walensky**

"Welcome back. We are live and taking your calls out of Orlando. But I want to go back to Robyn Walensky, WDBO. She's joining us where it all started. Where Caylee's remains were found rotting, animals having gnawed and displaced her tiny bones. Robyn Walensky, what's happening?"   **– HLN's Nancy Grace, July 18, 2011**

"Nancy, this is one of the saddest places on earth. You know I've been to a lot of crime scenes covering crime in the last twenty years, but this is it. Whoever put the body here, triple-bag little Caylee just down the block from the Anthony home, never wanted her to be found.

Robyn Walensky reporting for HLN's Nancy Grace Show
At woods scene July 18, 2011
Photo Courtesy: CNN

I want to just read very quickly, especially to your viewers, Nancy, who are parents and grandparents. There's a little postcard here from Chicago. And it's written by a little boy by the name of Jake. And he says, 'Sorry, you won't be able to see this.' And what he means is all these happy birthday balloons. See this sign somebody left this. 'Justice has failed but judgment remains.' And you know what, Nancy? Little Caylee won't be able to see it, but you know what, the world is here to see it. She was so loved. So loved, Nancy. It is so sad here."

– Robyn Walensky on HLN's Nancy Grace, July 18, 2011

"Robyn Walensky joining us from WDBO. As always, accurate reporting except for one major fact, Robyn, and to Jake in Chicago. She sees."
– HLN's Nancy Grace, July 18, 2011

"Nancy's poignant words give me chills, even though I am totally overheated and sunburnt from standing in the scalding hot Orlando summer sun. Amazingly, at my WDBO radio e-mail address the next day I get a note from the mother of the boy who purchased that postcard in Chicago, wrote on it, and placed it at the swamp scene."
– Robyn Walensky

"Hi, Robyn, I saw your clip on Nancy Grace last night about the postcard my son Jake Berry placed in a basket on July 11. I was so excited for him when I heard his name. That was amazing. Jake and I knew that when we were landing in Orlando that morning my mom wanted to stop by the memorial. Jake really wanted to leave something for her so while in O'Hare airport Jake picked out this postcard and thought it was so sad she'd never be able to come to Chicago. During this week while we visited our family, he attended vacation Bible school all week. Then out of the blue he said to me one day, 'Mom, even though what Casey did was wrong, God says we should forgive her.' That's a tough pill to swallow for me but he is right. We leave for Chicago tomorrow evening. Thank you so much for your lovely news report."
– Dean Berry Joliet, Illinois, sent Tuesday, July 19, 2011, 12:17 p.m.

"My final takeaway from the trial—the antics and chaos outside the Orange County Courthouse, which will forever disturb me. We are all here because a two-year-old is murdered and left to decompose in a swamp. This is lost on some of the spectators who act like they're in line to get on a ride at an amusement park. This is not Disney, this is a Courthouse. On most days I arrive in the 3:00 a.m. or 4:00 a.m. hour to keep tabs on the line, get audio, and report how many tourists and locals are showing up to wait for tickets. The length of the line depends on who is expected to testify. George Anthony, get ready for a long line. Some sleep out on the street overnight.

Others bring blankets, lawn chairs, plenty of snacks, and cards to pass the time. I interview folks from foreign countries, a woman from London, another from the Netherlands, here in Orlando to see Mickey at Disney and Casey in court. They are drawn to the case from far, far away. There are regulars in line, locals like "neck brace man" (an injured guy who's off the job who always wears a neck brace to court), the "Sharpie lady," and the "Sharpie lady sub.," They patrol the long line and try to keep order during the endless overnight hours as hundreds of spectators wait for the fifty open seats per day allotted to the public.

"Sharpie Lady Sub" numbering people's hands
in line as spectators wait for seats
Photo Courtesy: Robyn Walensky

The "Sharpie gals," a woman who comes up with the idea, and her "sub" on the days she not there, take turns writing a number with a black magic marker on everyone's right hand to affirm his or her place in line. The reason, outsiders not familiar with their 'system' would often try to cut, which results in chaos and fights. One morning a lady is pushed and falls. She is hauled off on stretcher into an ambulance and sent off to the hospital.

EMT's tend to spectator knocked to ground while waiting in line for
a ticket to get into the Casey Anthony Trial
Photo Courtesy: Robyn Walensky

On another morning, there is a massive fight because people were again 'cutting' the line and one guy ends up in a headlock. Police are called to the scene to break it up, but no one is arrested. Lost in all the cheering and daily picture taking of the lawyers and the Anthony's arriving for court is the fact a totally innocent child was triple bagged and tossed in a swamp. On many days I am disgusted watching these spectators act like animals. As for Casey Anthony... she is found "Not Guilty" by a jury of her peers, but no one is saying she's totally "innocent" and had nothing to do with her daughter's demise. Immediately after the verdict, a doctored picture of Casey and OJ Simpson circulates on Facebook and the Internet. At first glance I laugh. But then I don't. I am reminded a Los Angeles jury finds OJ "not guilty" at his murder trial. Simpson gets away with killing his ex-wife, Nicole Brown Simpson, and her friend Ron Goldman. He is found guilty at the second civil trial but never fully pays what he owes literally and figuratively. No money can ever replace people. At this writing Simpson sits in prison after being convicted on felony charges in the Vegas casino caper…and I believe Karma may catch up with Casey Anthony too.   **– Robyn Walensky**

Protestor outside courthouse wears Karma t-shirt

Photo Courtesy: Robyn Walensky

ACKNOWLEDGMENTS

I would like to thank: Cox Media Group, WDBO Radio FM 96.5 & AM 580 Newstalk Orlando, general manager Susan Larkin, program director Steve Holbrook, news director Marsha Taylor, assistant news director and morning anchor Bob Hazen, morning host Jim Turner, the team who pulled together the WDBO nightly Casey on Trial show, anchor and co-host Dave Wahl, Orlando attorney Sherri Dewitt, and assistant program director Levi May, CNN Headline News, Nancy Grace, the entire team at the Nancy Grace show, and producer/booker Beth Carey. I would like to thank Nikki Namadar for transcribing and Deborah Guidry for computer assistance. This book would not be possible without the cooperation of the Orange County Sheriff's Office, Sheriff Jerry Demings, public information officer Captain Angelo Nieves, Corporal Yuri Melich, Detective John Allen, crime scene supervisor Michael Vincent, CSI Geraldo Bloise, CSI Alina Burroughs, CSI Jennifer Welch, and Deputy Jason Forgey. I would also like to acknowledge the assistance of Danielle Tavernier at the state attorney's office who assisted with photographs, and documents. On a personal note, I would like to acknowledge my parents, Dr. Norman and Susan Walensky, who have always encouraged me to follow my deep passion for reporting, my grandmother Sally Walensky, whose spirit lives on in my heart. Her message to be there for people equally on the dark days as well as the sunny ones is ever present in my daily existence. And I would like to thank retired New Orleans Police Sergeant Bobby Guidry, my rock, whose passion for protecting people and passion for police work is an inspiration.

ABOUT THE AUTHOR

Robyn Walensky
Photo Courtesy: Robyn Walensky

Robyn Walensky is a veteran news reporter and anchor who has been covering crime, terrorism, politics, and breaking news for more than twenty years in both radio and television. She was in two terrorist attacks, and reported extensively on the World Trade Center bombing in 1993, the federal trial of the WTC 93 Plotters, and September 11th. She is co-editor/author of the book Covering Catastrophe—Broadcast Journalists Report 9-11-01. Walensky has a BA in journalism and political science from the George Washington University and an MA in journalism from New York University. She is a graduate of The Institute on Political Journalism at Georgetown University. She has taught Journalism courses at Tulane University in the classroom and online. Most recently, Walensky was the morning drive reporter covering the Casey Anthony Trial for WDBO Radio in Orlando, Florida, and a frequent guest on CNN's Nancy Grace Show. Walensky was the first female morning drive co-host on Rush Radio WRNO 99.5 FM in New Orleans. While at WGNO-TV in New Orleans she reported extensively on the Gulf oil spill and the run-up to the Saints winning their first Super Bowl. Walensky was a national correspondent and anchor for Fox News Radio, covering the JonBenet Ramsey case, the deaths of Anna Nicole Smith and her son in the Bahamas, the disappearance of Natalee Holloway in Aruba, OJ Simpson's arrest and trial in Las Vegas, and countless other crime and terrorism stories such as the shooting at VA Tech, and the Fort Dix 6. Earlier in her career, she also reported for AP Radio, WWOR-TV, and 1010 WINS Radio in New York. Walensky was born in New Brunswick, New Jersey, and went to Millburn Senior High School. Currently Walensky works for Mercury Radio Arts. She is anchor/reporter for The Blaze and can be heard daily on Glenn Beck's national radio show. rwalensky@aol.com, Facebook: robyn walensky, Twitter: @robynwalensky

13482346R00094

Made in the USA
Charleston, SC
13 July 2012